Amazon Pinpoint User Guide

A catalogue record for this book is available from the Hong Kong Public Libraries.

Published in Hong Kong by Samurai Media Limited.

Email: info@samuraimedia.org

ISBN 9789888408115

Contents

What Is Amazon Pinpoint?

Amazon Pinpoint is an AWS service that you can use to engage with your customers across multiple messaging channels. You can send push notifications, emails, or text messages (SMS), depending on the purpose of your campaign.

This section describes the major features of Amazon Pinpoint.

Define Audience Segments

Reach the right audience for your messages by defining audience segments. A segment designates which users receive the messages that are sent from a campaign. You can define dynamic segments based on data that's reported by your application, such as operating system or mobile device type. You can also import static segments that you define outside of Amazon Pinpoint.

Engage Your Audience with Messaging Campaigns

Engage your audience by creating a messaging campaign. A campaign sends tailored messages on a schedule that you define. You can create campaigns that send mobile push, email, or SMS messages.

To experiment with alternative campaign strategies, set up your campaign as an A/B test, and analyze the results with Amazon Pinpoint analytics.

Send Direct Messages

Keep your customers informed by sending direct mobile push and SMS messages—such as new account activation messages, order confirmations, and password reset notifications—to specific users.

Analyze User Behavior

Gain insights about your audience and the effectiveness of your campaigns by using the analytics that Amazon Pinpoint provides. You can view trends about your users' level of engagement, purchase activity, and demographics. You can monitor your message traffic with metrics for messages sent and opened. Through the Amazon Pinpoint API, your application can report custom data, which Amazon Pinpoint makes available for analysis.

To analyze or store the analytics data outside of Amazon Pinpoint, you can configure Amazon Pinpoint to stream the data to Amazon Kinesis.

Get Started

Get started with Amazon Pinpoint by creating a project in AWS Mobile Hub. Your Mobile Hub project becomes available in Amazon Pinpoint. For more information, see Getting Started with Amazon Pinpoint.

Currently, Amazon Pinpoint is available in the US East (N. Virginia) Region.

Getting Started with Amazon Pinpoint

To begin using Amazon Pinpoint, add a project to AWS Mobile Hub. Then, choose your project in the Amazon Pinpoint console to define user segments, create push notification campaigns, and view analytics.

Adding a Project to Amazon Pinpoint

Before you can use Amazon Pinpoint, you must create a project in the AWS Mobile Hub console at https://console.aws.amazon.com/mobilehub/.

Mobile Hub is an AWS service that helps you create and configure mobile app backend features and integrate them into your app. When you create your project, add the **Messaging & Analytics** feature. After you create the project in Mobile Hub, it becomes available in Amazon Pinpoint.

When you add the **Messaging & Analytics** feature, you choose one or more messaging channels to enable. After you create a project that supports at least one channel, you can manage channel settings, or enable other channels, in the Amazon Pinpoint console. For more information about creating a project and enabling a specific channel, see:

- Setting up Amazon Pinpoint Mobile Push Channels
- Setting up the Amazon Pinpoint Email Channel
- Setting up the Amazon Pinpoint SMS Channel

Getting Started with Amazon Pinpoint

After you add a project to Amazon Pinpoint, you can choose your project in the Amazon Pinpoint console at https://console.aws.amazon.com/pinpoint/ to do the following tasks.

1. Define a user segment so that you can engage a specific subset of your audience with a messaging campaign.

2. Create a campaign to send tailored messages to your segment according to a schedule that you define.

3. View analytics to learn how many users your campaign is sending messages to, how many users are viewing those messages, and other information.

Amazon Pinpoint Channels

A *channel* represents the platform through which you engage your audience segment with messages. For example, to send messages to your mobile app users, you must have an Amazon Pinpoint project in which the *mobile push* channel is enabled. Amazon Pinpoint supports the following channel types:

- Mobile push
- Email
- SMS

Before you can use Amazon Pinpoint to engage your audience, you must create an Amazon Pinpoint project, and that project must support one or more channels. To add a new project to Amazon Pinpoint, create a project using AWS Mobile Hub, and add the **Messaging & Analytics** feature to the project. After you create a project in Mobile Hub, it becomes available in Amazon Pinpoint.

After you create a project and enable a channel, you can use your project to send messages. You can define the audience segment that you want to engage and then define a campaign that sends messages to that segment. Or, to quickly send a message to a limited audience, you can send a direct message without creating a campaign.

- Amazon Pinpoint Mobile Push Channels
- Amazon Pinpoint Email Channel
- Amazon Pinpoint SMS Channel

Amazon Pinpoint Mobile Push Channels

With Amazon Pinpoint, you can engage your mobile app users by sending push notifications through a mobile push channel. You can send push notifications to Android and iOS apps using separate channels for the following push notification services:

- Firebase Cloud Messaging (FCM) or its predecessor, Google Cloud Messaging (GCM).

- Apple Push Notification service (APNs)

- Baidu Cloud Push

- Amazon Device Messaging (ADM)

To enable mobile push channels, you must first define your app as a project in AWS Mobile Hub. Then, integrate your app with Amazon Pinpoint.

- Setting up Amazon Pinpoint Mobile Push Channels
- Monitoring Mobile Push Activity with Amazon Pinpoint
- Managing Mobile Push Channels with Amazon Pinpoint

Setting up Amazon Pinpoint Mobile Push Channels

Before you can use Amazon Pinpoint to send push notifications to your app, you must define your app as a project in AWS Mobile Hub and integrate your app with Amazon Pinpoint. Mobile Hub is an AWS service that helps you create and configure mobile app backend features and integrate them into your app.

When you define your project in Mobile Hub, you set up channels for Firebase Cloud Messaging (FCM), Google Cloud Messaging (GCM), or Apple Push Notification service (APNs). To set up channels for Baidu Cloud Push or Amazon Device Messaging (ADM), manage your channels using the **Settings** page for your project in the Amazon Pinpoint console.

If you don't already have an app that is enabled for Amazon Pinpoint, see the following information in the *Amazon Pinpoint Developer Guide*:

- Setting Up Push Notifications for Amazon Pinpoint – Provides steps to create and download the required credentials from the Apple Developer website or the Google Firebase console.

- Getting Started: Creating an App With Amazon Pinpoint Support – Provides steps for adding your app as a project in AWS Mobile Hub and integrating your app with Amazon Pinpoint.

After you add an app to Amazon Pinpoint, you can update your push notification credentials on the **Settings** page. For more information, see Managing Mobile Push Channels with Amazon Pinpoint.

Monitoring Mobile Push Activity with Amazon Pinpoint

For push notifications that you send as part of a campaign, Amazon Pinpoint provides options for monitoring your mobile push activity.

Note
To monitor push notification activity, you must use a campaign. You cannot monitor push notification activity outside of a campaign.

Streaming Mobile Push Event Data

To monitor data, such as successful and failed mobile push deliveries, configure Amazon Pinpoint to stream mobile push event data to Amazon Kinesis Data Streams or Amazon Kinesis Data Firehose. Then, you can use the Kinesis platform to analyze this push data. For more information, see Streaming Amazon Pinpoint Events to Kinesis.

For examples of the event data that Amazon Pinpoint streams to Kinesis, see Event Data in the *Amazon Pinpoint Developer Guide*.

Amazon Pinpoint Analytics

The **Analytics** page in the Amazon Pinpoint console shows trends related to user engagement, campaign outreach, revenue, and more. To monitor your mobile push activity, you can view metrics such as:

Targeted
User devices to which Amazon Pinpoint attempted to deliver messages.

Delivered
The number of successful message deliveries.

Delivery rate
The percentage of all delivery attempts that were successful.

Total opened
The number of app openings resulting from users tapping notifications sent by the campaign.

Open rate
Percentage of recipients who opened your app after receiving a push notification from a campaign.

Opt out rate
Percentage of users who chose not to receive push notifications for your app.

For more information, see Amazon Pinpoint Analytics.

Managing Mobile Push Channels with Amazon Pinpoint

Using the console, you can update the credentials that allow Amazon Pinpoint to send push notifications to iOS and Android devices. You can provide credentials for the following push notification services, each of which is supported by an Amazon Pinpoint channel:

- Firebase Cloud Messaging (FCM) or its predecessor, Google Cloud Messaging (GCM).
- Apple Push Notification service (APNs).
- Baidu Cloud Push.
- Amazon Device Messaging (ADM).

For FCM, GCM, and APNs, you initially provide your credentials when you add your app as a mobile project in AWS Mobile Hub. For Baidu and ADM, you can provide your credentials only in the Amazon Pinpoint console.

To update mobile push settings

1. Sign in to the AWS Management Console and open the Amazon Pinpoint console at https://console.aws. amazon.com/pinpoint/.

2. On the **Projects** page, choose the project for which you want to manage mobile push settings.

3. In the navigation menu, choose **Settings**.

4. On the **Settings** page, choose **Channels**, and choose **Mobile Push**.

5. Under **Choose the push notification services that you want to enable**, you can update your credentials for the following services:

   - **FCM/GCM** – Requires an API key (also referred to as a server key), which you get from the Firebase console or the Google API console. For more information about getting FCM credentials, see Credentials in the Firebase documentation.

   - **APNs** – Requires an authentication token signing key or a TLS certificate, which you get from your Apple developer account. For more information, see the *Managing APNs Settings* section.

   - **Baidu** – Requires an API key and a secret key, which you get from your Baidu Cloud Push project.

   - **ADM** – Requires the OAuth Credentials (Client ID and Client Secret) from your Amazon Developer account. For more information, see Obtaining Amazon Device Messaging Credentials in the Amazon Developer documentation.

6. When you finish, choose **Save**.

Managing APNs Settings

On the **Settings** page, for **APNs**, you can authorize Amazon Pinpoint to send push notifications to your iOS app by providing information about your APNs *key* or *certificate*:

Key
A private signing key used by Amazon Pinpoint to cryptographically sign APNs authentication tokens. You obtain the signing key from your Apple developer account.
If you provide a signing key, Amazon Pinpoint uses a token to authenticate with APNs for every push notification that you send. With your signing key, you can send push notifications to APNs production and sandbox environments.
Unlike certificates, your signing key does not expire. You only provide your key once, and you don't need to renew it later. You can use the same signing key for multiple apps. For more information, see Communicate with APNs using authentication tokens in *Xcode Help*.

Certificate

A TLS certificate that Amazon Pinpoint uses to authenticate with APNs when you send push notifications. An APNs certificate can support both production and sandbox environments, or it can support only the sandbox environment. You obtain the certificate from your Apple developer account.

A certificate expires after one year. When this happens, you must create a new certificate, which you then provide to Amazon Pinpoint to renew push notification deliveries. For more information, see Communicate with APNs using a TLS certificate in *Xcode Help*.

To manage APNs settings

1. For **Default authentication type**, choose whether Amazon Pinpoint authenticates with APNs using your signing **key** or your TLS **certificate**. Amazon Pinpoint uses this default for every APNs push notification that you send using the console. You can override the default when you send a message programmatically using the Amazon Pinpoint API, the AWS CLI, or an AWS SDK. If your default authentication type fails, Amazon Pinpoint does not attempt to use the other authentication type.

2. For **Authentication type**, choose **Key** or **Certificate** to manage the settings for that type.

   - For **Key**, provide the following information from your Apple developer account at https://developer.apple.com/account/. Amazon Pinpoint requires this information to construct authentication tokens.

     - **Key ID** – The ID assigned to your signing key. To find this value, choose **Certificates, IDs & Profiles**, and choose your key in the **Keys** section.

     - **Bundle identifier** – The ID assigned to your iOS app. To find this value, choose **Certificates, IDs & Profiles**, choose **App IDs** in the **Identifiers** section, and choose your app.

     - **Team ID** – The ID assigned to your Apple developer account team. This value is provided on the **Membership** page.

     - **Authentication key** – The .p8 file that you download from your Apple developer account when you create an authentication key. Apple allows you to download your authentication key only once.

   - For **Certificate**, provide the following information:

     - **SSL certificate** – The .p12 file for your TLS certificate. You can export this file from Keychain Access after you download and install your certificate from your Apple developer account.

     - **Certificate password** – If you assigned a password to your certificate, specify it here.

3. If your certificate supports sending push notifications to the APNs production environment, enable **certificate supports production environment**. Do not enable this option if your certificate supports only the sandbox environment.

4. When you finish, choose **Save**.

Amazon Pinpoint Email Channel

To engage your user segment with an email campaign, enable the email channel in Amazon Pinpoint.

You can create an Amazon Pinpoint project with email support by creating a project in AWS Mobile Hub and adding the **Messaging & Analytics** feature. You can also enable the email channel in an existing project by using the **Settings** page in the Amazon Pinpoint console. Before you send email with Amazon Pinpoint, you must verify that you own the *from* address or the email domain.

When you first enable the email channel, your AWS account has access only to the email sandbox. With sandbox access, you can send 200 emails per 24-hour period at a maximum rate of one email per second. You can only send emails to addresses you verify. To increase your sending limits and to send email to unverified email addresses, see Requesting Production Access for Email.

You can monitor your email activity by viewing analytics in the Amazon Pinpoint console or by streaming email events to Kinesis.

As your email needs change, you can manage your email channel by updating your email address or domain, or requesting a sending limits increase.

- Setting up the Amazon Pinpoint Email Channel
- Monitoring Email Activity with Amazon Pinpoint
- Managing the Amazon Pinpoint Email Channel

Setting up the Amazon Pinpoint Email Channel

To set up the Amazon Pinpoint email channel, you create a project in AWS Mobile Hub, enable the email channel for that project, and verify your email address or domain.

When you enable the email channel for the first time, Amazon Pinpoint does not immediately provide production access for email messaging. Instead, your AWS account has access only to the email sandbox, which imposes restrictions on your email traffic. To gain production access, submit a sending limit increase request through AWS Support.

- Creating an Amazon Pinpoint Project with Email Support
- Email Address or Domain Verification
- Domain Verification TXT Records
- Requesting Production Access for Email

Creating an Amazon Pinpoint Project with Email Support

You can create a new project with email support by using AWS Mobile Hub. In the Mobile Hub console, create a project, and add the **Messaging & Analytics** feature. Then, enable the email channel as part of that feature. After you create a project in Mobile Hub, the project becomes available in Amazon Pinpoint.

You can also enable the email channel for an existing Amazon Pinpoint project by using the **Settings** page in the Amazon Pinpoint console. For more information, see Updating Email Settings.

To create a project with email support

1. Sign in to the AWS Management Console and open the Mobile Hub console at https://console.aws.amazon.com/mobilehub.

2. If you have other Mobile Hub projects, choose **Create new mobile project**. If this is your first project, skip this step because you are taken directly to the page for creating a new project.

3. Enter a project name. The name you enter will be the name of your project in the Amazon Pinpoint console.

4. For the region, keep **US East (Virginia)**.

5. Choose **Create project**. Mobile Hub creates the project and shows the **Pick and configure features for your project** page.

6. Choose **Messaging & Analytics**.

7. On the **Messaging & Analytics** page, for **What engagement features do you want to enable?**, choose **Messaging**.

8. For **What Messaging Channels do you want to enable?**, choose **Email**.

9. For **Do you want to enable email messaging?**, choose **Enable**.

10. To verify your email address or domain, choose the **Amazon Pinpoint console** link. You are directed to the **Settings** page in the Amazon Pinpoint console, where you complete the following steps:

    1. Choose the email identity that you want to use: **Email address** or **Email domain**.

    2. Provide your email address or domain, and choose **Verify**. Then, follow the instructions displayed by the console.

       If you verify an email address, Amazon Pinpoint sends a verification email to the address that you provide. Follow the instructions in the email to complete the verification process.

       If you verify an email domain, the console displays a TXT record that you must add to the domain's DNS settings. For more information, see Domain Verification TXT Records.

       For more information on verifying an email address or domain, see Email Address or Domain Verification.

    3. When you finish, choose **Save**.

11. In the Mobile Hub console, for **What engagement features do you want to enable?**, choose **Analytics**, and choose **Enable**. With analytics enabled, Amazon Pinpoint provides metrics about your email campaign activity.

Email Address or Domain Verification

To confirm that you own an email address or domain, and to prevent others from using it, you must verify the address or domain.

Email Address Verification

When verifying your email address, consider the following:

- You can verify up to 10,000 identities (domains and email addresses, in any combination) per AWS account.

- You can apply labels to verified email addresses by adding a plus sign (+) and a string of text after the recipient's user name, and before the @ sign. For example, to add *label1* to the address *user@example.com*, use the modified address *user+label1@example.com*. You can use an unlimited number of labels on each verified address. You can use labels in the From and Return-Path fields to implement Variable Envelope Return Path (VERP). For more information about VERP, see http://en.wikipedia.org/wiki/Variable_envelope_return_path. **Note**
  When you verify an unlabeled address, you are verifying all addresses that could be formed by adding a label to the address. However, if you verify a labeled address, you cannot use other labels with that address.

Domain Verification

Before you can use Amazon Pinpoint to send emails from a domain, verify your domain to confirm that you own it and to prevent others from using it. When you verify an entire domain, you are verifying all email addresses from that domain, so you don't need to verify email addresses from that domain individually. For example, if you verify the domain example.com, you can send email from user1@example.com, user2@example.com, or any other user at example.com.

When verifying your domain, consider the following:

- You can send from any subdomain of the verified domain without specifically verifying the subdomain. For example, if you verify example.com, you do not need to verify a.example.com or a.b.example.com. As specified in RFC 1034, each DNS label can have up to 63 characters and the whole domain name must not exceed a total length of 255 characters.

- You can verify as many as 10,000 identities (domains and email addresses, in any combination) per AWS account.

Domain Verification TXT Records

Your domain is associated with a set of Domain Name System (DNS) records that you manage through your DNS provider. A TXT record is a type of DNS record that provides additional information about your domain. Each TXT record consists of a name and a value.

When you initiate domain verification using the Amazon Pinpoint console or API, Amazon Pinpoint gives you the name and value to use for the TXT record. For example, if your domain is *example.com*, the TXT record settings that Amazon Pinpoint generates look similar to the following example.

Name	Type	Value
_amazonses.example.com	TXT	pm-BGN/7MjnfhTKUZ06Enqq1PeGUaOkw8lG fcHU=

Add a TXT record to your domain's DNS server using the specified **Name** and **Value**. Amazon Pinpoint domain verification is complete when Amazon Pinpoint detects the existence of the TXT record in your domain's DNS settings.

If your DNS provider does not allow DNS record names to contain underscores, you can omit *_amazonses* from the **Name**. In that case, for the preceding example, the TXT record name would be *example.com* instead of *_amazonses.example.com*. To make the record easier to recognize and maintain, you can optionally prefix the **Value** with *amazonses:*. In the previous example, the value of the TXT record would therefore be *amazonses:pmBGN/7MjnfhTKUZ06Enqq1PeGUaOkw8lGhcfwefcHU=*.

Requesting Production Access for Email

We use a sandbox environment to help protect our customers from fraud and abuse. The sandbox environment also helps you establish your sender reputation with ISPs and email recipients. New Amazon Pinpoint email user accounts are placed in the sandbox environment. While your account is in the sandbox, you have full access to Amazon Pinpoint email sending methods, with the following restrictions:

- You can only send email from verified addresses and domains.
- You can only send email to addresses that you have verified, or to addresses associated with the mailbox simulator.
- You can send a maximum of 200 messages per 24-hour period.
- You can send a maximum of one message per second.

To remove these restrictions, see Opening a Sending Limits Increase Case.

Monitoring Email Activity with Amazon Pinpoint

For emails that you send as part of a campaign, Amazon Pinpoint provides options for monitoring your email activity.

Note
To monitor email activity, you must use a campaign. You cannot monitor email activity outside of a campaign.

Streaming Email Event Data

To monitor data, such as successful and failed email deliveries, configure Amazon Pinpoint to stream email event data to Amazon Kinesis Data Streams or Amazon Kinesis Data Firehose. Then, you can use the Kinesis platform to analyze this email data. For more information, see Streaming Amazon Pinpoint Events to Kinesis.

For examples of the event data that Amazon Pinpoint streams to Kinesis, see Event Data in the *Amazon Pinpoint Developer Guide*.

Amazon Pinpoint Analytics

On the **Analytics** page in the Amazon Pinpoint console, you can view metrics for the number of active targetable users that you can engage with the email channel.

Managing the Amazon Pinpoint Email Channel

You have the following options for managing your email channel with Amazon Pinpoint:

- To enable the email channel for an existing project, or to update your email address or domain, you can use the Amazon Pinpoint console.

- To increase your email sending limits, you can open a Sending Limits Increase case with AWS Support.

- Updating Email Settings

- Managing Email Sending Limits

Updating Email Settings

Use the Amazon Pinpoint console to update the email settings for your project. You can enable the email channel for an existing project, or you can update your email address or domain.

To set up a new project with email support, see Creating an Amazon Pinpoint Project with Email Support.

To update your email settings

1. Sign in to the AWS Management Console and open the Amazon Pinpoint console at https://console.aws. amazon.com/pinpoint/.

2. On the **Projects** page, choose the project for which you want to update email settings.

3. In the navigation menu, choose **Settings**.

4. On the **Settings** page, choose **Channels**, and then choose **Email**.

5. If you haven't already, choose **Enable email channel**.

6. Choose the email identity that you want to add or update: **Email address** or **Email domain**.

7. Provide your email address or domain, and choose **Verify**. Then, follow the instructions displayed by the console.

   If you verify an email address, Amazon Pinpoint sends a verification email to the address that you provide. Follow the instructions in the email to complete the verification process.

   If you verify an email domain, the console displays a TXT record that you must add to the domain's DNS settings. For more information, see Domain Verification TXT Records.

   For more information on verifying an email address or domain, see Email Address or Domain Verification.

8. When you finish, choose **Save**.

Managing Email Sending Limits

To regulate the number of email messages that you can send and the rate at which you can send them, your AWS account has sending limits. Sending limits benefit all Amazon Pinpoint users because they help to maintain the trusted relationship between Amazon Pinpoint and Internet service providers (ISPs). Sending limits help you gradually ramp up your sending activity. They decrease the likelihood that ISPs will block your emails because of sudden, unexpected spikes in your email sending volume or rate.

The following are Amazon Pinpoint sending limits:

Sending Quota
The maximum number of emails that you can send in a 24-hour period. The sending quota reflects a rolling time period. Every time you try to send an email, Amazon Pinpoint checks how many emails you sent in the previous 24 hours. If the total number of emails that you have sent is less than your quota, your send request is accepted and your email is sent. If you have already sent your full quota, your send request is rejected with a throttling exception. For example, if your sending quota is 50,000, and you sent 15,000 emails in the previous 24 hours, then you can send another 35,000 emails right away. If you have already sent 50,000 emails in the previous 24 hours, you cannot send more emails until some of the previous sending rolls out of its 24-hour window.

Maximum Send Rate
The maximum number of emails that Amazon Pinpoint can accept from your account per second. You can exceed this limit for short bursts, but not for a sustained period of time.
The rate at which Amazon Pinpoint accepts your messages might be less than the maximum send rate.

When your account is in the Amazon Pinpoint sandbox, your sending quota is 200 messages per 24-hour period and your maximum sending rate is one message per second. To increase your sending limits, submit an Amazon Pinpoint Sending Limits Increase case. For more information, see Requesting Production Access for Email. After your account moves out of the sandbox and you start sending emails, you can increase your sending limits further by submitting another Amazon Pinpoint Sending Limits Increase case.

Increasing Your Sending Limits

When your account is out of the sandbox, your sending limits increase if you are sending high-quality content and we detect that your utilization is approaching your current limits. Often, the system automatically increases your quota before you need it, and no further action is needed.

If your existing quota is not adequate for your needs and the system did not automatically increase your quota, you can open an Amazon Pinpoint Sending Limits Increase case in AWS Support Center.

Important
Plan ahead. Be aware of your sending limits and try to stay within them. If you anticipate needing a higher quota than the system allocated, open an Amazon Pinpoint Sending Limits Increase case well before the date that you need the higher quota. If you anticipate needing to send more than one million emails per day, you must open an Amazon Pinpoint Sending Limits Increase case.

For Amazon Pinpoint to increase your quota, use the following guidelines:

- **Send high-quality content** – Send content that recipients want and expect.

- **Send real production content** – Send your actual production email. This enables Amazon Pinpoint to accurately evaluate your sending patterns, and verify that you are sending high-quality content.

- **Send near your current quota** – If your volume stays close to your quota without exceeding it, Amazon Pinpoint detects this usage pattern and can automatically increase your quota.

- **Have low bounce and complaint rates** – Try to minimize the numbers of bounces and complaints. High numbers of bounces and complaints can adversely affect your sending limits. **Important**
  Test emails that you send to your own email addresses may adversely affect your bounce and complaint

metrics, or appear as low-quality content to our filters. Whenever possible, use the Amazon Simple Email Service (Amazon SES) mailbox simulator to test your system. Emails that are sent to the mailbox simulator do not count toward your sending metrics or your bounce and complaint rates. For more information, see Testing Amazon SES Email Sending.

Opening a Sending Limits Increase Case

To apply for higher sending limits for Amazon Pinpoint, open a case in AWS Support Center by using the following instructions.

To request a sending limit increase

1. In your web browser, go to AWS Support Center. If you are not already signed in to the AWS Management Console, type your user name and password when prompted.

2. Choose **Create Case**.

3. Complete the sending limit increase request by providing the following information:

   - **Regarding** – Choose **Service Limit Increase**.

   - For **Limit Type** – Choose **Pinpoint**.

   - **Region** – Select the AWS Region for which you are requesting a sending limit increase. Your sending limits are separate for each AWS Region. For supported regions, see AWS Regions and Endpoints in the *AWS General Reference*.

   - **Limit** – Choose one of the following options:

     - Choose **Desired Daily Sending Quota** if you want to increase the number of messages you can send per day.

     - Choose **Desired Maximum Send Rate** if you want to increase the number of messages you can send per second.

   - **New limit value** – Enter the amount you are requesting. **Note**
     Only request the amount you think you'll need. We cannot guarantee that you will receive the amount you request. The larger your request, the more justification you need to provide to have your request granted.

   - **Mail type** – Choose the option that best represents your use case.

   - **Website URL** – Type the URL of your website. **Note**
     You are not required to provide a website URL. However, providing a website URL helps us evaluate your request.

   - **My email-sending complies with the AWS Service Terms and AWS Acceptable Use Policy (AUP)** – Select **Yes** or **No**.

   - **I only send to recipients who have specifically requested my mail** – Select **Yes** or **No**.

   - **I have a process to handle bounces and complaints** – Select **Yes** or **No**.

   - **Use Case Description** – Describe how you plan to send email using Amazon Pinpoint in as much detail as possible. For example, describe the type of emails you are sending and how email sending fits into your business. The more information you provide that indicates that you send high-quality messages to recipients who want and expect them, the more likely we are to approve your request.

   - For **Support Language**, choose the language in which you want to communicate with the AWS Support team.

   - For **Contact method**, choose **Web**.

4. When you finish, choose **Submit**.

Checking the Status of Your Request

After you submit your request, we review your case. Allow one full business day for processing.

To check the status of your sending limit increase request

1. In your web browser, go to AWS Support Center. If you are not already signed in to the AWS Management Console, type your user name and password when prompted.

2. In the navigation panel on the left side of the screen, choose **Dashboard**.

3. Under **Recent Cases**, choose your sending limit increase request case.

4. Review the messages in the **Correspondence** section. The messages in this section tell you if your request was accepted or rejected. If your request was accepted, the message specifies your daily and per-second sending limits.

If your account is currently in the email sandbox, and if you are granted a sending limit increase, your account is automatically taken out of the sandbox. After your account is out of the sandbox, you can send email to non-verified addresses. However, you must still verify your sending addresses and domains.

Over time, we will gradually increase your sending limits. If your needs exceed the gradual increase, you can open another Amazon Pinpoint Sending Limits Increase request.

Amazon Pinpoint SMS Channel

You can enable the SMS channel in Amazon Pinpoint to send text messages, or *SMS messages*, to SMS-enabled devices.

For many use cases, you must enable SMS options with AWS Support before you use Amazon Pinpoint to send SMS messages. For example, to enable two-way SMS, you must first obtain a dedicated origination number from AWS Support.

You can manage SMS channel settings for your use case and budget. For example, you can specify your monthly spending limit, and you can define keywords and responses for two-way SMS.

Note
Your SMS channel settings apply to all SMS messages that you send from your AWS account. This includes messages sent with AWS services other than Amazon Pinpoint.

Where required by local laws and regulations (such as the US and Canada), SMS recipients can opt out, which means that they choose to stop receiving SMS messages from your AWS account.

You can use Amazon Pinpoint to send SMS messages to more than 200 countries and/or regions. For more information, see Supported Countries and Regions.

- Setting up the Amazon Pinpoint SMS Channel
- Requesting Support for SMS Messaging with Amazon Pinpoint
- Monitoring SMS Activity with Amazon Pinpoint
- Managing the Amazon Pinpoint SMS Channel
- Supported Countries and Regions
- SMS Best Practices

Setting up the Amazon Pinpoint SMS Channel

To send SMS messages with Amazon Pinpoint, you need an Amazon Pinpoint project in which the SMS channel is enabled. If your project is based on a mobile app, create it by using AWS Mobile Hub. Otherwise, create your project by using the AWS CLI.

You can also enable the SMS channel for an existing project by using the **Settings** page in the Amazon Pinpoint console. For more information, see Managing the Amazon Pinpoint SMS Channel.

Creating an SMS Project With AWS Mobile Hub

You can enable SMS messaging for a mobile app by creating a project with AWS Mobile Hub. In the Mobile Hub console, create a project, and add the **Messaging & Analytics** feature. Then, enable the SMS channel as part of that feature. After you create a project in Mobile Hub, the project becomes available in Amazon Pinpoint.

For more information, see the following topics in the *AWS Mobile Developer Guide*:

- To create a project in Mobile Hub, see Get Started.
- After you create a project, to enable SMS messaging, see Add Messaging to Your Mobile App with Amazon Pinpoint.

Creating an SMS Project With the AWS CLI

You can create an Amazon Pinpoint project that is enabled for SMS messaging by using the AWS Command Line Interface (AWS CLI). The AWS CLI requires Python 2 version 2.6.5 or later, or Python 3 version 3.3 or later. For more information about installing and configuring the AWS CLI, see Installing the AWS Command Line Interface in the *AWS Command Line Interface User Guide*.

To create an project that is enabled for SMS, use the `create-app` and `update-sms-channel` commands, as shown by the following examples.

Example create-app command
Use the http://docs.aws.amazon.com/cli/latest/reference/pinpoint/create-app.html command to create an Amazon Pinpoint project:

```
1 $aws pinpoint create-app --create-application-request Name="My SMS Project"
```

The following response is shown in the terminal:

```
1 {
2     "ApplicationResponse": {
3         "Id": "1a2b3c4d5e6f7g8h9i0j1k2l3m4n5o6",
4         "Name": "My SMS Project"
5     }
6 }
```

Note the ID provided in the response because you will use it when you enable the SMS channel.

Example update-sms-channel command
Use the http://docs.aws.amazon.com/cli/latest/reference/pinpoint/update-sms-channel.html command to enable the SMS channel for a project:

```
1 $aws pinpoint update-sms-channel --application-id application-id --sms-channel-request Enabled=
      true
```

The following response is shown in the terminal:

```
1  {
2      "SMSChannelResponse": {
3          "ApplicationId": "1a2b3c4d5e6f7g8h9i0j1k2l3m4n5o6",
4          "CreationDate": "2018-02-20T22:15:05.025Z",
5          "Enabled": true,
6          "Id": "sms",
7          "IsArchived": false,
8          "LastModifiedDate": "2018-02-20T22:15:05.025Z",
9          "Platform": "SMS",
10         "Version": 1
11     }
12 }
```

After you create a project, it is available in the Amazon Pinpoint console at https://console.aws.amazon.com/pinpoint/.

Next Steps

You've created a project that is enabled for SMS messaging. Now you can use Amazon Pinpoint to send SMS messages.

To engage an audience segment with an SMS campaign, see Engage Your Audience with Messaging Campaigns.

To send an SMS message directly to a limited audience without creating a campaign, see Direct Messages with Amazon Pinpoint.

Some SMS options, such as dedicated origination numbers or sender IDs, are unavailable until you contact AWS Support. For more information, see Requesting Support for SMS Messaging with Amazon Pinpoint.

Requesting Support for SMS Messaging with Amazon Pinpoint

Certain SMS options with Amazon Pinpoint are unavailable until you contact AWS Support. Open a case in the AWS Support Center to request any of the following:

-

An increase to your monthly SMS spend threshold

By default, the monthly spend threshold is 1.00 USD. Your spend threshold determines the volume of messages that you can send with Amazon Pinpoint. Request a spend threshold that meets the expected monthly message volume for your SMS use case.

-

A dedicated number (short code or long code)

Your dedicated origination number is assigned to your AWS account, and it's available exclusively to you. If you don't have a dedicated number, Amazon Pinpoint assigns a number to your messages. This number is shared with other Amazon Pinpoint users, and it varies based upon destination and message type (transactional or promotional). By reserving a short code or long code, you can send your messages with a persistent origination number. This makes it easier for your audience to recognize that your organization is the source of your messages. A dedicated long code or short code is required if you want to enable two-way SMS with Amazon Pinpoint. Long codes are supported only for two-way SMS.

-

A dedicated sender ID

A *sender ID* is a custom ID that is shown as the sender on the recipient's device. For example, you can use your business brand to make the message source easier to recognize. Support for sender IDs varies by country and/or region. For more information, see Supported Countries and Regions.

When you create your case in the AWS Support Center, include all the information that's required for the type of request you're submitting. Otherwise, AWS Support contacts you to obtain this information before proceeding. By submitting a detailed case, you help ensure that your case is fulfilled without delays. For the details that are required for specific types of SMS requests, see the following topics.

- Requesting Increases to Your Monthly SMS Spend Threshold for Amazon Pinpoint
- Requesting Dedicated Short Codes for SMS Messaging with Amazon Pinpoint
- Requesting Dedicated Long Codes for SMS Messaging with Amazon Pinpoint
- Requesting Sender IDs for SMS Messaging with Amazon Pinpoint

Requesting Increases to Your Monthly SMS Spend Threshold for Amazon Pinpoint

Your monthly spend threshold sets how much you can spend each calendar month on SMS messaging when you use Amazon Pinpoint. When Amazon Pinpoint determines that sending an SMS message would incur a cost that exceeds your spend threshold for that month, it stops publishing SMS messages within minutes.

Important

Because Amazon Pinpoint is a distributed system, it stops sending SMS messages within a time interval of minutes of the spend limit being exceeded. During that interval, if you continue to send SMS messages, you might incur costs that exceed your limit.

By default, the spend threshold is 1.00 USD. For information about SMS pricing, see Amazon Pinpoint Pricing.

Typically, AWS Support processes your case within 2 business days. Depending on the spend limit you request and the complexity of your case, AWS Support might require an additional 3–5 days to ensure that your request can be processed.

To request a spend threshold increase, complete the following steps.

Step 1: Open an Amazon Pinpoint SMS Case

Open a case with AWS Support by completing the following steps.

1. Sign in to the AWS Management Console, and go to the AWS Support Center.
2. Choose **Create case**.
3. For **Regarding**, choose **Service Limit Increase**.
4. For **Limit Type**, choose **Pinpoint SMS**.

Step 2: Specify Your Request

Tell AWS Support that you're requesting a spend threshold increase by completing the following steps.

1. For **Resource Type**, choose **General Limits**.
2. For **Limit**, choose **Account Spend Threshold Increase**.
3. For **New limit value**, type the maximum amount in USD that you'll spend on SMS messages each calendar month.
4. (Optional) If you want to include multiple requests in this support case, choose **Add another request**. Then, specify the type of request.

   If you include multiple requests, provide the required information for each. For the required information, see the other sections within Requesting Support for SMS Messaging with Amazon Pinpoint.

Step 3: Describe Your SMS Use Case

Describe how you use SMS messaging by completing the following steps.

1. For **Link to site or app which will be sending SMS**, identify the website or application where your audience members will opt in to receive your SMS messages.
2. For **Type of messages**, choose the type of SMS message that you send:

- **Transactional** – Important informational messages that support customer transactions, such as order confirmations or transaction alerts. Transactional messages must not contain promotional content.

- **Promotional** – Noncritical messages that promote your business or service, such as special offers or announcements.

- **One Time Passwords** – Messages that provide passwords to authenticate with your website or application.

3. For **Targeted Countries**, specify the countries that you send SMS messages to. For more information, see Supported Countries and Regions.

   If your list of countries exceeds the character limit for this text box, you can instead specify your countries in the **Use Case Description** box.

4. For **Use Case Description**, provide the following details:

   - The website or app of the company or service that's sending SMS messages.

   - The service that's provided by your website or app, and how your SMS messages contribute to that service.

   - How users sign up to voluntarily receive your SMS messages on your website, app, or other location.

   If your requested spend threshold (the value you specified for **New limit value**) exceeds 10,000 USD, provide the following additional details for each country that you're messaging:

   - Whether you're using a sender ID or short code. If you're using a sender ID, provide:

     - The sender ID.

     - Whether the sender ID is registered with wireless carriers in the country.

   - The maximum expected transactions-per-second (TPS) for your messaging.

   - The average message size.

   - The template for the messages that you send to the country.

   - (Optional) Character encoding needs, if any.

5. When you finish, choose **Submit**.

Step 4: Update Your SMS Settings in the Amazon Pinpoint Console

After AWS notifies you that your monthly spend threshold is increased, complete the following steps.

1. Sign in to the AWS Management Console and open the Amazon Pinpoint console at https://console.aws. amazon.com/pinpoint/.

2. On the **Projects** page, choose **Account settings**.

3. Under **General**, for **Account spending limit**, type the maximum amount, in USD, that you want to spend on SMS messages each calendar month. You can specify a value that's less than or equal to your total monthly spend threshold. By setting a lower value, you can control spending while retaining the capacity to scale up as needed.

4. Choose **Save**.

Requesting Dedicated Short Codes for SMS Messaging with Amazon Pinpoint

A short code is a five-digit or six-digit number that's meant for high-volume SMS messaging. Short codes are often used for application-to-person (A2P) messaging, two-factor authentication (2FA), and marketing.

To use short codes in multiple countries, request a separate short code for each country. You can use a short code only to message the same country in which it was approved by wireless carriers.

For information about short code pricing, see Amazon Pinpoint Pricing.

Important
If you're new to SMS messaging with Amazon Pinpoint, request a monthly SMS spend threshold that meets the expected demands of your SMS use case. By default, your monthly spend threshold is 1.00 USD. You can request to increase your spend threshold in the same support case that includes your request for a short code. Or, you can use a separate case. For more information, see Requesting Increases to Your Monthly SMS Spend Threshold for Amazon Pinpoint.

After receiving your request, AWS works with the wireless carriers to provision your short code on your behalf. This provisioning process takes 8–12 weeks.

To request a dedicated short code, complete the following steps.

Step 1: Open an Amazon Pinpoint SMS Case

Open a case with AWS Support by completing the following steps.

1. Sign in to the AWS Management Console, and go to the AWS Support Center.

2. Choose **Create case**.

3. For **Regarding**, choose **Service Limit Increase**.

4. For **Limit Type**, choose **Pinpoint SMS**.

Step 2: Specify Your Request

Tell AWS Support that you're requesting a dedicated short code by completing the following steps.

1. For **Resource Type**, choose **Dedicated SMS Short Codes**.

2. For **Limit**, choose the type of message that you'll send with your short code:

   - **One-time Passwords/Two-Factor Authentication** – Messages that provide passwords to authenticate with your website or application.

   - **Promotional/Marketing** – Noncritical messages that promote your business or service, such as special offers or announcements.

   - **Transactional** – Important informational messages that support customer transactions, such as order confirmations or transaction alerts. Transactional messages must not contain promotional content.

3. For **New limit value**, specify the number of short codes that you're requesting. Typically, this value is **1**.

4. (Optional) If you want to include multiple requests in this support case, choose **Add another request**. Then, specify the type of request.

   If you include multiple requests, provide the required information for each. For the required information, see the other sections within Requesting Support for SMS Messaging with Amazon Pinpoint.

Step 3: Describe Your SMS Use Case

Describe how you'll use your dedicated short code by completing the following steps.

1. For **Link to site or app which will be sending SMS**, identify the website or application where your audience members will opt in to receive your SMS messages.

2. For **Type of messages**, choose the type of message that you'll send using your short code: **Transactional**, **Promotional**, or **One Time Passwords**.

3. For **Targeted Countries**, specify the country that you'll send SMS messages to with your short code.

4. For **Use Case Description**, provide the following details, which AWS requires to register your short code with wireless carriers:

Company information:

- Company name.

- Company mailing address.

- Name and phone number for the primary contact for your request.

- Email address and toll-free number for support at your company.

- Company tax ID.

- Name of your product or service.

User sign-up process:

- Company website, or the website that your customers will sign up on to receive messages from your short code.

- How users will sign up to receive messages from your short code. Specify one or more of the following options:

  - **Text messages**.

  - **Website**.

  - **Mobile app**.

  - **Other**. If other, explain.

- The text for the option to sign up for messages on your website, app, or elsewhere.

- The sequence of messages that you'll use for double opt-in. Provide:

  1. The SMS message that you'll send when a user signs up. This message asks for the user's consent for recurring messages. For example:

     ExampleCorp: Reply YES to receive account transaction alerts. Msg&data rates may apply.

  2. The opt-in response that you expect from the user. This is typically a keyword, such as *YES*.

  3. The confirmation message that you'll send in response. For example:

     You are now registered for account alerts from ExampleCorp. Msg&data rates may apply. Txt STOP to cancel or HELP for info.

The purpose of your messages:

- The purpose of the messages that you'll send with your short code. Specify one of the following options:

  - **Promotions and marketing**.

  - **Location-based services**.

- **Notifications.**

- **Information on demand.**

- **Group chat.**

- **Two-factor authentication (2FA).**

- **Polling and surveys.**

- **Sweepstakes or contests.**

- **Other.** If other, explain.

- Whether you'll use your short code for promotional or marketing messages for a business other than your own.

Message content:

- The message that you'll send in response to the *HELP* keyword. This message must include customer support contact information. For example:

  For assistance with your account, call 1 (NNN) 555-0199.

- The message that you'll send in response to the *STOP* keyword. This message must confirm that messages are no longer sent to the user. For example:

  You are now opted out and will no longer receive messages.

- The text you'll use for a periodic reminder that the user is subscribed to your messages. For example:

  Reminder: You are subscribed to account alerts from ExampleCorp. Msg&data rates may apply. Txt STOP to cancel or HELP for info.

- An example of each type of message that you'll send with your short code.

- The frequency with which users will receive messages from your short code. For example, "3 messages per week".

1. When you finish, choose **Submit**.

Step 4: Update Your SMS Settings in the Amazon Pinpoint Console

After AWS notifies you that your short code is registered with the wireless carriers, complete the following steps.

1. Sign in to the AWS Management Console and open the Amazon Pinpoint console at https://console.aws.amazon.com/pinpoint/.

2. On the **Projects** page, choose **Account settings**.

3. Under **Number settings**, choose the short code that AWS assigned to your account.

4. Under **Keywords**, verify your keywords and responses. The console shows the keyword responses that you provided to AWS Support.

5. (Optional) If you want to specify additional keyword responses, or if you want to process inbound messages outside of Amazon Pinpoint, configure two-way SMS settings. For more information, see Two-Way SMS Settings.

6. When you finish making your changes, choose **Save**.

Next Steps

You've registered a short code with wireless carriers and reviewed your settings in the Amazon Pinpoint console. Now you can use Amazon Pinpoint to send SMS messages with your short code as the origination number.

To engage an audience segment with an SMS campaign, see Engage Your Audience with Messaging Campaigns.

To send an SMS message directly to a limited audience without creating a campaign, see Direct Messages with Amazon Pinpoint.

Requesting Dedicated Long Codes for SMS Messaging with Amazon Pinpoint

A long code (also referred to as a long virtual number, or LVN) is a standard 10-digit phone number. Long codes are meant for low-volume, person-to-person communication. For example, in the United States and Canada, sending rates for long codes are restricted to 1 TPS. Sending high-volume traffic to a long code might prompt wireless carriers to block the messages by blacklisting the long code. Long codes are useful for low-volume use cases, or for testing your SMS program before you scale up and request a short code. With Amazon Pinpoint, long codes are supported only for two-way SMS.

You can request up to 5 long codes for each country that you'll send SMS messages to.

Important
If you're new to SMS messaging with Amazon Pinpoint, request a monthly SMS spend threshold that meets the expected demands of your SMS use case. By default, your monthly spend threshold is 1.00 USD. You can request to increase your spend threshold in the same support case that includes your request for a long code. Or, you can submit a separate case. For more information, see Requesting Increases to Your Monthly SMS Spend Threshold for Amazon Pinpoint.

After receiving your request, AWS registers your long code in the targeted countries on your behalf. Typically, AWS Support processes your case within 2 business days. Depending on the complexity of your case, AWS Support might require an additional 3–5 days to ensure that your request can be processed.

To request a dedicated long code, complete the following steps.

Step 1: Open an Amazon Pinpoint SMS Case

Open a case with AWS Support by completing the following steps.

1. Sign in to the AWS Management Console, and go to the AWS Support Center.

2. Choose **Create case**.

3. For **Regarding**, choose **Service Limit Increase**.

4. For **Limit Type**, choose **Pinpoint SMS**.

Step 2: Specify Your Request

Tell AWS Support that you're requesting a dedicated long code by completing the following steps.

1. For **Resource Type**, choose **Dedicated SMS Long Codes**.

2. For **Limit**, choose the type of message that you'll send with your long code:

   - **One-time Passwords/Two-Factor Authentication** – Messages that provide passwords to authenticate with your website or application.

   - **Promotional/Marketing** – Noncritical messages that promote your business or service, such as special offers or announcements.

   - **Transactional** – Important informational messages that support customer transactions, such as order confirmations or transaction alerts. Transactional messages must not contain promotional content.

3. For **New limit value**, specify the number of long codes that you're requesting. Typically, this value is **1**. You can request up to 5 long codes for each country in your request.

4. (Optional) If you want to include multiple requests in this support case, choose **Add another request**. Then, specify the type of request.

   If you include multiple requests, provide the required information for each. For the required information, see the other sections in Requesting Support for SMS Messaging with Amazon Pinpoint.

Step 3: Describe Your SMS Use Case

Describe how you'll use your dedicated long code by completing the following steps.

1. For **Link to site or app which will be sending SMS**, identify the website or application where your audience members will opt in to receive your SMS messages.

2. For **Type of messages**, choose the type of message that you'll send using your long code: **Transactional**, **Promotional**, or **One Time Passwords**.

3. For **Targeted Countries**, specify the countries that you're requesting a long code for. For more information, see Supported Countries and Regions.

   If your list of countries exceeds the character limit for this text box, you can instead specify your countries in the **Use Case Description** box.

4. For **Use Case Description**, provide the following details:

   - The AWS Region where you'll use Amazon Pinpoint to send SMS messages with your long code.

   - Because long codes are supported only for two-way SMS, confirm that you require your long code for two-way SMS purposes.

5. When you finish, choose **Submit**.

Step 4: Update Your SMS Settings in the Amazon Pinpoint Console

After AWS notifies you that your long code is registered in the targeted countries, complete the following steps.

1. Sign in to the AWS Management Console and open the Amazon Pinpoint console at https://console.aws.amazon.com/pinpoint/.

2. On the **Projects** page, choose **Account settings**.

3. Under **Number settings**, choose the long code that AWS assigned to your account. The console shows the **Number settings** page for your long code. Under **Keywords**, the console provides:

   - The keywords HELP and STOP, and their default response messages. You can edit the response messages, but you can't edit the keywords.

   - The default registered keyword and its default response message. You can edit both of these values.

4. In the table that contains the keyword or response that you want to edit, choose **Edit**, and make your changes.

5. (Optional) If you want to specify additional keyword responses, or if you want to process inbound messages outside of Amazon Pinpoint, configure two-way SMS settings. For more information, see Two-Way SMS Settings.

6. When you finish making your changes, choose **Save**.

Next Steps

You've registered a long code and updated your settings in the Amazon Pinpoint console. Now you can use Amazon Pinpoint to send SMS messages with your long code as the origination number.

To engage an audience segment with an SMS campaign, see Engage Your Audience with Messaging Campaigns.

To send an SMS message directly to a limited audience without creating a campaign, see Direct Messages with Amazon Pinpoint.

Requesting Sender IDs for SMS Messaging with Amazon Pinpoint

A sender ID is a custom name that's displayed as the message sender on the receiving device. For example, you can use your business brand to make the message source easier to recognize.

Support for sender IDs varies by country or region. For example, messages delivered to U.S. phone numbers don't display the sender ID. For the countries and regions that support sender IDs, see Supported Regions and Countries.

Important
If you're new to SMS messaging with Amazon Pinpoint, request a monthly SMS spend threshold that meets the expected demands of your SMS use case. By default, your monthly spend threshold is 1.00 USD. You can request to increase your spend threshold in the same support case that includes your request for a sender ID. Or, you can use a separate case. For more information, see Requesting Increases to Your Monthly SMS Spend Threshold for Amazon Pinpoint.

To request a sender ID, complete the following steps.

Step 1: Open an Amazon Pinpoint SMS Case

Open a case with AWS Support by completing the following steps.

1. Sign in to the AWS Management Console, and go to the AWS Support Center.

2. Choose **Create case**.

3. For **Regarding**, choose **Service Limit Increase**.

4. For **Limit Type**, choose **Pinpoint SMS**.

Step 2: Specify Your Request

Tell AWS Support that you're requesting a sender ID by completing the following steps.

1. For **Resource Type**, choose **General Limits**.

2. For **Limit**, choose **SenderID Registration**.

3. For **New limit value**, type the number of sender IDs that you're requesting. Typically, this value is **1**.

4. (Optional) If you want to include multiple requests in this support case, choose **Add another request**. Then, specify the type of request.

   If you include multiple requests, provide the required information for each. For the required information, see the other sections in Requesting Support for SMS Messaging with Amazon Pinpoint.

Step 3: Describe Your SMS Use Case

Describe how you'll use your sender ID by completing the following steps.

1. For **Link to site or app which will be sending SMS**, identify the website or application where your audience members will opt in to receive your SMS messages.

2. For **Type of messages**, choose the type of message that you'll send using your sender ID:

   - **Transactional** – Important informational messages that support customer transactions, such as order confirmations or transaction alerts. Transactional messages must not contain promotional content.

- **Promotional** – Noncritical messages that promote your business or service, such as special offers or announcements.

- **One Time Passwords** – Messages that provide passwords to authenticate with your website or application.

3. For **Targeted Countries**, specify the countries where you want to register a sender ID. Support for sender IDs and sender ID registration requirements vary by country. For more information, see Supported Countries and Regions.

   If your list of countries exceeds the character limit for this text box, you can instead specify the countries in the **Use Case Description** box.

4. For **Use Case Description**, provide the following details:

   - The name of your organization (or the organization associated with the sender ID).

   - The sender ID to register. Typically, the sender ID can contain up to 11 alphanumeric characters, including at least one letter and no spaces. These requirements can vary depending on the country you're messaging.

   - How your sender ID relates to the name of your organization, if that relationship isn't clear. For example, if your sender ID is an acronym that includes your organization name when expanded, provide the expanded form.

   - The template for the messages that you'll send with the sender ID.

5. When you finish, choose **Submit**.

Step 4: Update Your SMS Settings in the Amazon Pinpoint Console

After AWS notifies you that your sender ID is registered in the targeted countries, complete the following steps.

1. Sign in to the AWS Management Console and open the Amazon Pinpoint console at https://console.aws.amazon.com/pinpoint/.

2. On the **Projects** page, choose **Account settings**.

3. Under **General**, for **Default sender ID**, type your sender ID.

4. Choose **Save**.

Next Steps

You've registered a sender ID and updated your settings in the Amazon Pinpoint console. Now you can use Amazon Pinpoint to send SMS messages with your sender ID. SMS recipients in supported countries will see your sender ID as the message sender on their devices.

To engage an audience segment with an SMS campaign, see Engage Your Audience with Messaging Campaigns.

To send an SMS message directly to a limited audience without creating a campaign, see Direct Messages with Amazon Pinpoint.

Monitoring SMS Activity with Amazon Pinpoint

Amazon Pinpoint provides the following options for monitoring your SMS activity.

Streaming SMS Event Data

To monitor your SMS activity, such as successful and failed message deliveries, you can configure Amazon Pinpoint to stream SMS event data to Amazon Kinesis Data Streams or Amazon Kinesis Data Firehose. Then, you can use the Kinesis platform to analyze your SMS data. For more information, see Streaming Amazon Pinpoint Events to Kinesis.

For examples of the event data that Amazon Pinpoint streams to Kinesis, see Event Data in the *Amazon Pinpoint Developer Guide*.

Amazon Pinpoint Analytics

On the **Analytics** page in the Amazon Pinpoint console, you can view metrics for the number of active targetable users that you can engage with the SMS channel.

Managing the Amazon Pinpoint SMS Channel

Use the Amazon Pinpoint console to enable the SMS channel and manage SMS settings, such as your default message type (transactional or promotional) and your monthly spending limit.

To update your SMS settings, use the **Account settings** page. For more information, see Managing Account Settings in Amazon Pinpoint.

Before you can use Amazon Pinpoint to send SMS messages, you must enable the SMS channel for one or more projects. To create a new project with SMS support, see Setting up the Amazon Pinpoint SMS Channel. To enable the SMS channel in an existing project, complete the following steps:

To enable the SMS channel for a project

1. Sign in to the AWS Management Console and open the Amazon Pinpoint console at https://console.aws. amazon.com/pinpoint/.

2. On the **Projects** page, choose the project for which you want to enable the SMS channel.

3. In the navigation menu, choose **Settings**.

4. On the **Settings** page, choose **Channels**, and then choose **SMS**.

5. Choose **Enable SMS channel**.

6. Choose **Save**.

SMS Opt Out

Where required by local laws and regulations (such as in the US and Canada), SMS recipients can use their devices to opt out by replying to the message with any of the following:

- ARRET (French)
- CANCEL
- END
- OPT-OUT
- OPTOUT
- QUIT
- REMOVE
- STOP
- TD
- UNSUBSCRIBE

To opt out, the recipient must reply to the same long code or short code that Amazon Pinpoint used to deliver the message. After opting out, the recipient no longer receives SMS messages from your AWS account.

Supported Countries and Regions

You can use Amazon Pinpoint to send SMS messages to the countries and regions listed in the following table. This table also lists the countries and regions that support sender IDs and two-way SMS.

Country or region	ISO code	Supports sender IDs	Supports two-way SMS
Afghanistan	AF		
Albania	AL	Yes	
Algeria	DZ		
Andorra	AD	Yes	
Angola	AO	Yes	
Anguilla	AI	Yes	
Antigua and Barbuda	AG	Yes	
Argentina	AR		Yes
Armenia	AM	Yes	
Aruba	AW	Yes	
Australia	AU	Yes	Yes
Austria	AT	Yes	Yes
Azerbaijan	AZ		
Bahamas	BS	Yes	
Bahrain	BH	Yes	
Bangladesh	BD		
Barbados	BB	Yes	
Belarus	BY	Yes	
Belgium	BE		Yes
Belize	BZ	Yes	
Benin	BJ	Yes	
Bermuda	BM	Yes	
Bhutan	BT	Yes	
Bolivia	BO	Yes	
Bosnia and Herzegovina	BA	Yes	
Botswana	BW	Yes	
Brazil	BR		Yes
Brunei	BN	Yes	
Bulgaria	BG	Yes	
Burkina Faso	BF	Yes	
Burundi	BI	Yes	
Cambodia	KH	Yes	
Cameroon	CM	Yes	
Canada	CA		Yes
Cape Verde	CV	Yes	
Cayman Islands	KY	No	
Central African Republic	CF	Yes	
Chad	TD	Yes	
Chile	CL		Yes
China	CN		Yes
Colombia	CO		
Comoros	KM	Yes	
Cook Islands	CK	Yes	
Costa Rica	CR		
Croatia	HR		Yes

Country or region	ISO code	Supports sender IDs	Supports two-way SMS
Cyprus	CY	Yes	
Czech Republic	CZ	Yes[1]	Yes
Democratic Republic of the Congo	CD		
Denmark	DK	Yes	Yes
Djibouti	DJ	Yes	
Dominica	DM	Yes	
Dominican Republic	DO		
East Timor	TL		
Ecuador	EC		
Egypt	EG	Yes	
El Salvador	SV		
Equatorial Guinea	GQ	Yes	
Estonia	EE	Yes	Yes
Ethiopia	ET		
Faroe Islands	FO	Yes	
Fiji	FJ	Yes	
Finland	FI	Yes	Yes
France	FR	Yes	Yes
French Guiana	GF		
Gabon	GA	Yes	
Gambia	GM	Yes	
Georgia	GE	Yes	
Germany	DE	Yes	Yes
Ghana	GH		
Gibraltar	GI	Yes	
Greece	GR	Yes	
Greenland	GL	Yes	
Grenada	GD	Yes	
Guadeloupe	GP	Yes	
Guam	GU		
Guatemala	GT		Yes
Guinea	GN	Yes	
Guinea-Bissau	GW	Yes	
Guyana	GY	Yes	
Haiti	HT	Yes	
Honduras	HN		Yes
Hong Kong	HK	Yes	Yes
Hungary	HU		Yes
Iceland	IS	Yes	
India	IN	Yes[1]	Yes
Indonesia	ID	Yes[1]	Yes
Iraq	IQ		
Ireland	IE	Yes	Yes
Israel	IL	Yes	Yes
Italy	IT	Yes	Yes
Ivory Coast	CI		
Jamaica	JM	Yes	
Japan	JP	Yes[2]	Yes
Jordan	JO	Yes[1]	
Kazakhstan	KZ		
Kenya	KE		

Country or region	ISO code	Supports sender IDs	Supports SMS	two-way
Kiribati	KI			
Kuwait	KW			
Kyrgyzstan	KG			
Laos	LA			
Latvia	LV	Yes	Yes	
Lebanon	LB	Yes		
Lesotho	LS	Yes		
Liberia	LR	Yes		
Libya	LY	Yes		
Liechtenstein	LI	Yes		
Lithuania	LT	Yes	Yes	
Luxembourg	LU	Yes		
Macau	MO	Yes		
Macedonia	MK	Yes		
Madagascar	MG	Yes		
Malawi	MW	Yes		
Malaysia	MY		Yes	
Maldives	MV	Yes		
Mali	ML			
Malta	MT	Yes		
Martinique	MQ	Yes		
Mauritania	MR	Yes		
Mauritius	MU	Yes		
Mexico	MX		Yes	
Moldova	MD	Yes		
Monaco	MC			
Mongolia	MO	Yes		
Montenegro	ME	Yes		
Montserrat	MS	Yes		
Morocco	MA			
Mozambique	MZ			
Myanmar	MM			
Namibia	NA			
Nepal	NP			
Netherlands	NL	Yes	Yes	
Netherlands Antilles	AN	Yes		
New Caledonia	NC	Yes		
New Zealand	NZ		Yes	
Nicaragua	NI			
Niger	NE	Yes		
Nigeria	NG	Yes[1]	Yes	
Norway	NO	Yes	Yes	
Oman	OM	Yes[1]		
Pakistan	PK			
Palau	PW			
Palestinian Territories	PS	Yes[1][3]		
Panama	PA			
Papua New Guinea	PG	Yes		
Paraguay	PY	Yes		
Peru	PE	No		
Philippines	PH	Yes[1]	Yes	
Poland	PL	Yes	Yes	

Country or region	ISO code	Supports sender IDs	Supports two-way SMS
Portugal	PT	Yes	Yes
Puerto Rico	PR		Yes
Qatar	QA		
Republic of the Congo	CG		
Reunion Island	RE	Yes	
Romania	RO		Yes
Russia	RU	Yes[1]	Yes
Rwanda	RW	Yes	
Saint Kitts and Nevis	KN		
Saint Lucia	LC		
Saint Vincent and the Grenadines	VC		
Samoa	WS	Yes	
Sao Tome and Principe	ST	Yes	
Saudi Arabia	SA	Yes[1]	
Senegal	SN	Yes	
Serbia	RS	Yes	
Seychelles	SC	Yes	
Sierra Leone	SL	Yes	
Singapore	SG	Yes	Yes
Slovakia	SK	Yes	Yes
Slovenia	SI	Yes	Yes
Solomon Islands	SB	Yes	
Somalia	SO	Yes	
South Africa	ZA		Yes
South Korea	KR		Yes
South Sudan	SS	Yes	
Spain	ES	Yes	Yes
Sri Lanka	LK		
Suriname	SR	Yes	
Swaziland	SZ	Yes	
Sweden	SE	Yes	Yes
Switzerland	CH	Yes	Yes
Taiwan	TW		Yes
Tajikistan	TJ	Yes	
Tanzania	TZ	Yes	
Thailand	TH	Yes	Yes
Togo	TG	Yes	
Tonga	TO	Yes	
Trinidad and Tobago	TT	Yes	
Tunisia	TN	Yes	
Turkey	TR		Yes
Turkmenistan	TM	Yes	
Turks and Caicos Islands	TC	Yes	
Uganda	UG	Yes	
Ukraine	UA	Yes	Yes
United Arab Emirates	AE	Yes[1]	
United Kingdom	GB	Yes	Yes
United States	US		Yes
Uruguay	UY		

Country or region	ISO code	Supports sender IDs	Supports two-way SMS
Uzbekistan	UZ	Yes	
Vanuatu	VU	Yes	
Venezuela	VE		
Vietnam	VN		
Virgin Islands, British	VG	Yes	
Virgin Islands, US	VI	Yes	
Yemen	YE	Yes	
Zambia	ZM	Yes	
Zimbabwe	ZW	Yes	

Notes

1. Senders are required to use a sender ID. To request a sender ID from AWS Support, see Requesting Sender IDs for SMS Messaging with Amazon Pinpoint.

2. All carriers in Japan except KDDI support sender ID.

3. Jawwal is the only carrier in the Palestinian Territories that supports alphabetic sender IDs.

Sender ID Support

The following table explains which ID is displayed when you send SMS messages to countries or regions where sender ID is supported, compared to those where sender ID isn't supported.

[See the AWS documentation website for more details]

SMS Best Practices

Mobile phone users tend to have a very low tolerance for unsolicited SMS messages. Response rates for unsolicited SMS campaigns will almost always be low, and therefore the return on your investment will be poor.

Additionally, mobile phone carriers continuously audit bulk SMS senders. They throttle or block messages from numbers that they determine to be sending unsolicited messages.

Sending unsolicited content is also a violation of the AWS Acceptable Use Policy. The Amazon Pinpoint team routinely audits SMS campaigns, and might throttle or block your ability to send messages if it appears that you're sending unsolicited messages.

Finally, in many countries, regions, and jurisdictions, there are severe penalties for sending unsolicited SMS messages. For example, in the United States, the Telephone Consumer Protection Act states that consumers are entitled to $500–$1,500 in damages (paid by the sender) for each unsolicited message that they receive.

This section describes several best practices that might help you improve your customer engagement and avoid costly penalties. However, you should always familiarize yourself with the customs and regulations in all of the jurisdictions where your customers are located before sending SMS messages through Amazon Pinpoint.

- Obtain Permission
- Audit Your Customer Lists
- Respond Appropriately
- Adjust Your Sending Based on Engagement
- Send at Appropriate Times
- Avoid Cross-Channel Fatigue
- Maintain Independent Lists
- Use Dedicated Short Codes

Obtain Permission

Don't send messages to customers who haven't asked to receive them.

If customers can sign up to receive your messages by using an online form, add a CAPTCHA to the form to prevent automated scripts from subscribing people without their knowledge.

When you receive an SMS opt-in request, send the customer a message that asks them to confirm that they want to receive messages from you. Don't send that customer any additional messages until they confirm their subscription. A subscription confirmation message might resemble the following example:

```
1 Text YES to join Example Corp. alerts. 2 msgs/month. Msg & data rates may apply.
2 Reply HELP for help, STOP to cancel.
```

Maintain records that include the date, time, and source of each opt-in request and confirmation. This might be useful if a carrier or regulatory agency requests it, and can also help you perform routine audits of your customer list.

Finally, note that transactional SMS messages, such as order confirmations or one-time passwords, typically don't require explicit consent as long as you tell your customers that you're going to send them these messages. However, you should never send marketing messages to customers who only provided you with permission to send them transactional messages.

Audit Your Customer Lists

If you send recurring SMS campaigns, audit your customer lists on a regular basis. Auditing your customer lists ensures that the only customers who receive your messages are those who are interested in receiving them.

When you audit your list, send each opted-in customer a message that reminds them that they're subscribed, and provides them with information about unsubscribing. A reminder message might resemble the following example:

```
1 You're subscribed to Example Corp. alerts. Msg & data rates may apply.
2 Reply HELP for help, STOP to unsubscribe.
```

Respond Appropriately

When a recipient replies to your messages, make sure that you respond with useful information. For example, when a customer responds to one of your messages with the keyword "HELP", send them information about the program that they're subscribed to, the number of messages you'll send each month, and the ways that they can contact you for more information. A HELP response might resemble the following example:

```
1 HELP: Example Corp. alerts: email help@example.com or call XXX-555-0199. 2 msgs/month.
2 Msg & data rates may apply. Reply STOP to cancel.
```

When a customer replies with the keyword "STOP", let them know that they won't receive any further messages. A STOP response might resemble the following example:

```
1 STOP: You're unsubscribed from Example Corp. alerts. No more messages will be sent.
2 Reply HELP, email help@example.com, or call XXX-555-0199 for more info.
```

Adjust Your Sending Based on Engagement

Your customers' priorities can change over time. If customers no longer find your messages to be useful, they might opt out of your messages entirely, or even report your messages as unsolicited. For these reasons, it's important that you adjust your sending practices based on customer engagement.

For customers who rarely engage with your messages, you should adjust the frequency of your messages. For example, if you send weekly messages to engaged customers, you could create a separate monthly digest for customers who are less engaged.

Finally, remove customers who are completely unengaged from your customer lists. This step prevents customers from becoming frustrated with your messages. It also saves you money and helps protect your reputation as a sender.

Send at Appropriate Times

Only send messages during normal daytime business hours. If you send messages at dinner time or in the middle of the night, there's a good chance that your customers will unsubscribe from your lists in order to avoid being disturbed. Furthermore, it doesn't make sense to send SMS messages when your customers can't respond to them immediately.

Avoid Cross-Channel Fatigue

In your campaigns, if you use multiple communication channels (such as email, SMS, and push messages), don't send the same message in every channel. When you send the same message at the same time in more than one channel, your customers will probably perceive your sending behavior to be annoying rather than helpful.

Maintain Independent Lists

When customers opt in to a topic, make sure that they only receive messages about that topic. Don't send your customers messages from topics that they haven't opted into.

Use Dedicated Short Codes

If you use short codes, maintain a separate short code for each brand and each type of message. For example, if your company has two brands, use a separate short code for each one. Similarly, if you send both transactional and promotional messages, use a separate short code for each type of message. To learn more about requesting short codes, see Requesting Dedicated Short Codes for SMS Messaging with Amazon Pinpoint.

Amazon Pinpoint Segments

A user *segment* represents a subset of your audience based on shared characteristics, such as how recently the users have used your application or which device platform they use. A segment designates who receives the messages delivered by a campaign. Define segments so that you can reach the right audience when you want to invite users back to your application, make special offers, or otherwise increase user engagement and purchasing.

You can add segments to Amazon Pinpoint in either of the following ways:

- Building segments by choosing selection criteria that is based on data that your application reports to Amazon Pinpoint.

- Importing segments that you defined outside of Amazon Pinpoint.

After you create a segment, you can use it in one or more campaigns. A campaign delivers tailored messages to the users in the segment.

- Building Segments
- Importing Segments
- Managing Segments

Building Segments

To reach the intended audience for a campaign, build a segment based on the data reported by your application.

For example, to reach users who haven't used your mobile app recently, you can define a segment for users who haven't used your app in the last 7 days.

User segments are defined by various criteria, including but not limited to:

- How recently they used your application
- The operating system they use
- The model of mobile device they use

Because the segment is built from segmentation criteria, it is dynamic, meaning the end users who belong to the segment vary over time based on user activity. For example, if your segment includes users who haven't used your application recently, users who respond to a campaign by using your application are removed from the segment.

To create a static segment, which includes a fixed set of end users, import endpoints that represent those users. For more information, see Importing Segments.

You can create segments separately from campaigns to assemble a collection of segments for multiple campaigns. You also can create a segment when creating a campaign.

To create a segment

1. Sign in to the AWS Management Console and open the Amazon Pinpoint console at https://console.aws. amazon.com/pinpoint/.
2. On the **Projects** page, choose the project to which you want to add the segment.
3. In the navigation menu, choose **Segments**. The **Segments** page opens, which displays previously defined segments and the number of active users that belong to them.
4. Choose **New segment**.
5. For **Segment name**, type a name for your segment to make it easy to recognize later.
6. For **How would you like to define your segment**, keep **Build segment** selected.

7. For **What messaging channel do you want to use?**, choose the channel you will use to engage the segment with a campaign. The channel must be enabled in your Amazon Pinpoint project. For more information, see Amazon Pinpoint Channels.
8. If you selected **Mobile push** as the channel type, define the **App usage criteria**. Select which users belong to the segment based on whether they have (or haven't) used your app within the specified number of days.

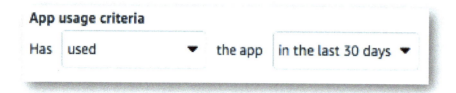

9. (Optional) For **Filter by standard attributes**, define which users belong to the segment based on the characteristics that are standard to Amazon Pinpoint.

10. (Optional) For **Filter by custom attributes** and **Filter by user attributes**, define which users belong to the segment based on custom attributes that you add to your Amazon Pinpoint endpoint resources.

11. When you are finished selecting criteria, choose **Create segment**.

Importing Segments

In Amazon Pinpoint, you can define a user segment by importing information about the users who belong to the segment.

Importing segments is useful if you have segments of your users outside of Amazon Pinpoint but you want to engage your users with Amazon Pinpoint campaigns.

Unlike the dynamic segments that you create with the segment builder in the console, an imported segment is an unchanging set of *endpoints*. Each endpoint is a unique messaging destination, such as an email address, a mobile device identifier, or a mobile phone number. When Amazon Pinpoint sends a message to the segment, it sends the message to each of the endpoints in that segment.

To import a file, you first upload it to an Amazon Simple Storage Service (Amazon S3) bucket. Next, you provide Amazon Pinpoint with the name of the Amazon S3 bucket that contains the file. Amazon Pinpoint retrieves the file from Amazon S3 and adds each endpoint in the file to a segment.

Creating Endpoint Files

You can define one or more endpoints in a CSV or newline-delimited JSON file, and then import that file into Amazon Pinpoint to create a segment.

When you import segments, consider the following:

- If you're importing new endpoints, the `Address` and `ChannelType` attributes are required.
- If you're updating existing endpoints, the `Id` attribute is required for each endpoint that you want to update.
- Amazon Pinpoint can't import compressed files.
- The files that you import must use UTF-8 character encoding.
- Your endpoint definitions can only include certain attributes. For a list, see Available Attributes.
- To determine if an endpoint is already registered, you can issue an HTTP `GET` request to the `endpoints` URI in the Amazon Pinpoint API.

The following two sections provide examples of JSON and CSV file layouts based on the data in the following table.

ChannelType	Address	Location.Country	Demo-graphic.Platform	Demo-graphic.Make
SMS	2065550182	USA	Android	LG
APNS	1a2b3c4d5e6f7g8h9i	USA	iOS	Apple
EMAIL	john.stiles@ example.com	CAN	iOS	Apple
GCM	4d5e6f1a2b3c4d5e6f	EGY	Android	Google
EMAIL	wang.xiulan@ example.com	CHN	Android	OnePlus

JSON Endpoint File Example

Amazon Pinpoint can import files in newline-delimited JSON format. In this format, each line is a complete JSON object that contains an individual endpoint definition, as in the following example:

```
1  {"ChannelType":"SMS","Address":"2065550182","Location":{"Country":"USA"},"Demographic": {"
       Platform":"Android","Make":"LG"}}
2  {"ChannelType":"APNS","Address":"1a2b3c4d5e6f7g8h9i0j1a2b3c4d5e6f","Location":{"Country":"USA
       "},"Demographic": {"Platform":"iOS","Make":"Apple"}}
3  {"ChannelType":"EMAIL","Address":"john.stiles@example.com","Location":{"Country":"CAN"},"
       Demographic": {"Platform":"iOS","Make":"Apple"}}
4  {"ChannelType":"GCM","Address":"4d5e6f1a2b3c4d5e6f7g8h9i0j1a2b3c","Location":{"Country":"EGY"},"
       Demographic": {"Platform":"Android","Make":"Google"}}
5  {"ChannelType":"EMAIL","Address":"wang.xiulan@example.com","Location":{"Country":"CHN"},"
       Demographic": {"Platform":"Android","Make":"OnePlus"}}
```

CSV Endpoint File Example

Amazon Pinpoint can also import endpoints that are defined in a CSV file, as in the following example:

```
1  ChannelType,Address,Location.Country,Demographic.Platform,Demographic.Make
2  SMS,2065550182,USA,Android,LG
3  APNS,1a2b3c4d5e6f7g8h9i0j1a2b3c4d5e6f,USA,iOS,Apple
4  EMAIL,john.stiles@example.com,CAN,iOS,Apple
5  GCM,4d5e6f1a2b3c4d5e6f7g8h9i0j1a2b3c,EGY,Android,Google
6  EMAIL,wang.xiulan@example.com,CHN,Android,OnePlus
```

The first line is the header, which contains the endpoint attributes. These attributes are the same as those in the endpoint JSON format. Use a period to address attributes that are nested in the JSON structure. For example, the header for the device make is `Demographic.Make`. The subsequent lines define the endpoints by providing values for each attribute in the header.

To include a comma, line break, or double quote in a value, enclose the value in double quotes, as in `"aaa ,bbb"`. For more information about the CSV format, see RFC 4180 Common Format and MIME Type for Comma-Separated Values (CSV) Files.

Uploading Endpoint Definitions to Amazon S3

Amazon S3 is an AWS service that provides highly scalable cloud storage. Amazon S3 stores data as objects within buckets, and those objects can be grouped into folders.

Before you import a segment, you must create an S3 bucket and upload your endpoint file to that bucket. You can organize the endpoints for different segments into separate folders. When Amazon Pinpoint imports the endpoints for a segment, it includes the endpoints within all folders and subfolders that belong to the Amazon S3 location you specify.

For an introduction to creating buckets and uploading objects, see the Amazon Simple Storage Service Getting Started Guide.

Amazon Pinpoint can import endpoints that are contained in the following types of files:

- Newline-delimited JSON
- Comma-separated values (CSV)

Amazon Pinpoint can import only one of these formats per segment, so the Amazon S3 path you specify should only contain one format type.

Importing a Segment

You can create a segment by importing the segment's endpoints from Amazon S3.

To import a segment

1. Sign in to the AWS Management Console and open the Amazon Pinpoint console at https://console.aws.amazon.com/pinpoint/.

2. On the **Projects** page, choose the project that you want to add the segment to.

3. In the navigation menu, choose **Segments**. The **Segments** page opens, which displays previously defined segments and the number of active users that belong to them.

4. Choose **New segment**.

5. For **Segment name**, type a name for your segment to make it easy to recognize later.

6. For **How would you like to define your segment**, choose **Import segment**.

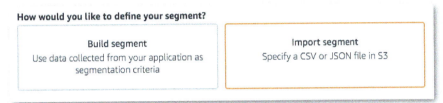

7. For **Amazon S3 URL**, type the location of the Amazon S3 bucket that contains the endpoints for your segment. The address of the bucket must be in the following format:

```
1 s3://bucket-name/folder-name
```

Amazon Pinpoint imports endpoints from the path you specify and from any subfolders in that path.

8. For **IAM role**, complete one of the following steps:

   - If you want to have Amazon Pinpoint create a role that allows it to read from an Amazon S3 bucket, select **Automatically create a role**. Then, for **Name for new role**, type a name for the role that you're creating.

   - If you've already created an IAM role that allows Amazon Pinpoint to read from an Amazon S3 bucket, select **Choose a role from your account**. Then, for **Role**, choose a role that contains the appropriate permissions.

9. For **What is the format of the file**, choose either **CSV** or **JSON**, depending on the format of your endpoint file.

10. Choose **Import Segment**. Amazon Pinpoint imports the endpoints from the specified Amazon S3 bucket and adds them to your segment.

    The **Jobs** page provides the status of your import. Refresh your browser to see the current status.

Available Attributes

The following table contains the list of attributes that you can specify in the files you import into Amazon Pinpoint. If you import segments using CSV files, the headers in the file should match the names shown in the **Attributes** column.

For JSON files, a period in the attribute name indicates that the name following the period is an object that is nested in a parent object with a name equal to the value preceding the period. For example, a JSON file that contains the `Demographic.Make` and `Demographic.Model` attributes has the following structure:

```
1 {
2 ...
3 "Demographic": {
4  ...
5  "Make":"Apple",
6  "Model":"iPhone"
7  ...
8  }
9 ...
10 }
```

You can replace attribute names shown in italics with any value. For example, you can create custom attributes called `User.UserAttributes.FirstName` and `User.UserAttributes.LastName`.

Attribute	Description
Address	The unique destination of the endpoint, such as an email address, a mobile phone number, or a token for mobile push notifications.
Attributes.custom_attribute	Custom attributes that your app reports to Amazon Pinpoint. You can use these attributes as selection criteria when you create a segment. You can replace custom_attribute with any value. You can specify up to 20 custom attributes per endpoint.
ChannelType	The channel type of the endpoint. Acceptable values: GCM, APNS, SMS, or EMAIL.
Demographic.AppVersion	The version number of the application associated with the endpoint.
Demographic.Locale	The locale of the endpoint in ISO 15897 format. For example, en_US (English language locale for the United States) or zh_CN (Chinese locale for China).
Demographic.Make	The manufacturer of the endpoint device, such as Apple or Samsung.
Demographic.Model	The model of the endpoint device, such as iPhone.
Demographic.ModelVersion	The model version of the endpoint device.
Demographic.Platform	The operating system of the endpoint device, such as ios or android.
Demographic.PlatformVersion	The platform version of the endpoint device.
Demographic.Timezone	The time zone of the endpoint. Specified as a tz database value, such as America/Los_Angeles.
EffectiveDate	The time at which the endpoint was last updated, in ISO 8601 format. For example, 20171011T150548Z.

Attribute	Description
Id	The unique ID of the endpoint.
Location.City	The city where the endpoint is located.
Location.Country	The three-letter code for the country or region where the endpoint is located, in ISO 3166-1 alpha-3 format. For example, USA (United States) or CHN (China). For a complete list of ISO 3166-1 alpha-3 abbreviations, see https://www.iso.org/obp/ui/#search/code.
Location.Latitude	The latitude of the endpoint location, rounded to one decimal place.
Location.Longitude	The longitude of the endpoint location, rounded to one decimal place.
Location.PostalCode	The postal or ZIP code of the endpoint.
Location.Region	The region of the endpoint location, such as a state or province.
Metrics.custom_attribute	Custom metrics, such as the number of sessions or number of items left in a cart, to use for segmentation purposes. You can replace custom_attribute with any value. You can specify up to 20 custom attributes per endpoint.These custom values can only be numeric. Because they are numeric, Amazon Pinpoint can perform arithmetic operations, such as average or sum, on them.
OptOut	Indicates whether a user has opted out of receiving messages. Acceptable values: ALL (user has opted out of all messages) or NONE (user has not opted out and receives all messages).
RequestId	The unique ID of the most recent request to update the endpoint.
User.UserAttributes.custom_attribute	Custom attributes that are specific to the user. You can replace custom_attribute with any value, such as FirstName or Age. You can specify up to 20 custom attributes per endpoint.
User.UserId	The unique ID of the user.

Note

You can specify up to 20 custom attributes per endpoint for `Attributes`, `Metrics`, and `User.UserAttributes`. However, you can create no more than 40 custom attributes across your entire Amazon Pinpoint account.

Managing Segments

You can use the Amazon Pinpoint console to create new segments, update the settings for existing segments, duplicate segments, delete segments, and more.

To manage a segment

1. Sign in to the AWS Management Console and open the Amazon Pinpoint console at https://console.aws.amazon.com/pinpoint/.

2. On the **Projects** page, choose the project that you want to manage segments for.

3. On the navigation menu, choose **Segments**.

4. On the **Segments** page, choose the segment that you want to manage.

On the **Segment** page, for a segment that's built from segmentation criteria, you can do the following:

- **Create campaign** – Create a campaign that uses the segment you're managing.

- **Copy to new** – Copy the segment to use its settings as a template for a new segment, in which you can change or keep any of the original settings.

- **Edit segment** – Change any of the segment's settings, such as the segmentation criteria that define which users belong to the segment.

- **Delete segment** – Remove the segment from Amazon Pinpoint. The segment becomes unavailable for future campaigns, but preexisting campaigns that use the segment are unaffected.

For an imported segment, you can do the following:

- **Create campaign** – Create a campaign that uses the segment you're managing.

- **Reimport segment** – Update the segment with the endpoint files that are currently stored in the Amazon S3 location that you originally imported the segment from.

- **Delete segment** – Remove the segment from Amazon Pinpoint. The segment becomes unavailable for future campaigns, but preexisting campaigns that use the segment are unaffected.

Amazon Pinpoint Campaigns

A *campaign* is a messaging initiative that engages a specific audience segment. A campaign sends tailored messages according to a schedule that you define. You can use the console to create a campaign that sends messages through any single channel that is supported by Amazon Pinpoint: mobile push, email, or SMS.

For example, to help increase engagement between your mobile app and its users, you could use Amazon Pinpoint to create and manage push notification campaigns that reach out to users of that app. Your campaign might invite users back to your app who haven't run it recently or offer special promotions to users who haven't purchased recently.

Your campaign can send a message to all users in a segment, or you can allocate a holdout, which is a percentage of users who receive no messages. The segment can be one that you created on the **Segments** page or one that you define while you create the campaign.

You can set the campaign's schedule to send the message once or at a recurring frequency, such as once a week. To prevent users from receiving the message at inconvenient times, the schedule can include a quiet time during which no messages are sent.

To experiment with alternative campaign strategies, set up your campaign as an A/B test. An A/B test includes two or more treatments of the message or schedule. Treatments are variations of your message or schedule. As your users respond to the campaign, you can view campaign analytics to compare the effectiveness of each treatment.

If you want to send a one-time message without engaging a user segment or defining a schedule, you can simply send a direct message instead of creating a campaign.

- Step 1: Begin a New Campaign
- Step 2: Specify the Audience Segment for the Campaign
- Step 3: Write the Message
- Step 4: Set the Campaign Schedule
- Step 5: Review and Launch the Campaign
- Managing Campaigns

Step 1: Begin a New Campaign

Use the Amazon Pinpoint console to create a campaign. You will:

- Choose the messaging channel (mobile push, email, or SMS).

- Choose the user segment for the campaign.

- Write the message.

- Define the schedule on which the campaign runs.

Optionally, you can set up your campaign as an A/B test to experiment with different treatments of the message or schedule. As users respond to your campaign, you can view campaign analytics to compare the effectiveness of each treatment.

To begin creating a campaign

1. Sign in to the AWS Management Console and open the Amazon Pinpoint console at https://console.aws. amazon.com/pinpoint/.

2. On the **Projects** page, choose the project for which you want to create a campaign.

3. In the navigation menu, choose **Campaigns**. The **Campaigns** page opens, and it displays summary information for previously defined campaigns.

4. Choose **New campaign**. The **Create a campaign** page opens at the **Details** step.

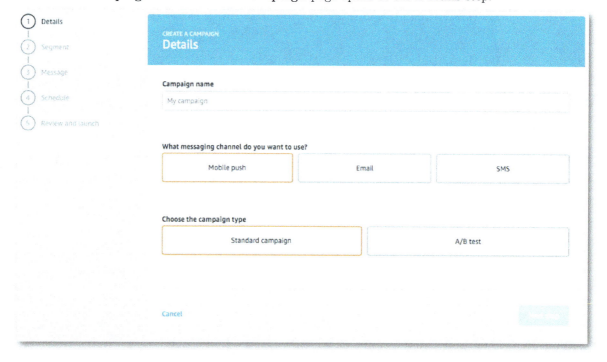

5. For **Campaign name**, type a name to make the campaign easy to recognize later.

6. For **What messaging channel do you want to use?**, choose the channel you will use to deliver your message. The channel must be enabled in your Amazon Pinpoint project. For more information, see Amazon Pinpoint Channels.

7. For **Choose the campaign type**, choose one of the following:

- **Standard campaign** – Sends a custom message to a specified segment according to a schedule that you define.

- **A/B Test** – Behaves like a standard campaign, but enables you to define different treatments for the campaign's message or schedule.

8. If you choose to create an A/B test, for **Choose what you will test for**, choose whether you will test variations of the campaign's **Messages** or **Schedule**.

Choose the campaign type

Standard campaign	A/B test

Choose what you will test

Messages	Schedule

9. Choose **Next step**.

Next
Step 2: Specify the Audience Segment for the Campaign

Step 2: Specify the Audience Segment for the Campaign

When creating a campaign, you can specify which audience segment to reach with your campaign by creating a new segment or choosing one that was previously created.

Prerequisite
Before you begin, complete Step 1: Begin a New Campaign.

To specify a segment

- For the **Segment** step in **Create a campaign**, specify a segment in one of the following ways:

    - Choose **Create a new segment** and follow the steps under *To build a segment*.

    - Choose **Use a previously defined segment** and select the segment that you want to target. Then, choose **Next step**.

To build a segment

To build your segment, define the segmentation criteria. As you choose criteria, the **Segment estimate** shows how many users the segment includes.

1. For **Name your segment to reuse it later**, type a name to make your segment easy to recognize.

2. If you selected **Mobile push** as the channel type, define the **App usage criteria**. Select which users belong to the segment based on whether they have (or haven't) used your app within the specified number of days.

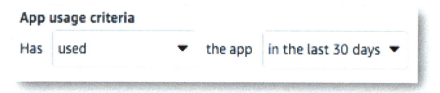

3. (Optional) For **Filter by standard attributes**, define which users belong to the segment based on the characteristics that are standard to Amazon Pinpoint.

4. (Optional) For **Filter by custom attributes** and **Filter by user attributes**, define which users belong to the segment based on custom attributes that you add to your Amazon Pinpoint endpoint resources.

5. If you chose to create a standard campaign, you can use this page to allocate the **holdout**, which is the percentage of users in the segment who will not receive messages from the campaign.

If you're creating an A/B test, you allocate the holdout when you define the message or schedule.

6. When you finish defining the segment, choose **Next step**.

Next
Step 3: Write the Message

Step 3: Write the Message

Write the message that your campaign delivers to your audience segment. If you chose to create a standard campaign, you write a single message, which you can revise after you launch the campaign.

If you chose to create an A/B test for your campaign's message, you define two or more *treatments*, which are variations of your message that the campaign sends to different portions of the segment. You cannot revise your treatments after you launch the campaign.

Prerequisite
Before you begin, complete Step 2: Specify the Audience Segment for the Campaign.

Writing a Mobile Push Message

If you chose **Mobile push** as the channel type, write the push notification that your campaign sends to your user segment, and choose the action that occurs when a user opens the notification.

Choose the notification type

- Choose the type of notification that your campaign delivers:

- **Standard notification** – A push notification with a title and message. Users are alerted by their mobile devices when they receive the notification.

- **Silent notification** – A custom JSON attribute-value pair that Amazon Pinpoint sends to your app without alerting users. Use silent notifications to send data that your app code is designed to receive and handle, for example to update the app's configuration or to show messages in the app.

To write a standard notification

1. If you previously saved a template that you want to use for your message, load it by choosing **Load template**. The **Title** and **Message** are populated with the contents of the template.

2. For **Title**, type the title you want to display above the message.

3. For **Message**, type the message body. Your push notification can have up to 200 characters. A character counter below the right edge of the field counts down from 200 as you enter the text of the message.

   When you finish writing your message, you can save it as a template for later use by choosing **Save as template**.

4. (Optional) For **Time To Live**, specify the length of time (in seconds) that the message is stored by the push notification services to which Amazon Pinpoint sends the message. These services can include Apple Push Notification service (APNs), Firebase Cloud Messaging (FCM), and Google Cloud Messaging (GCM).

   While storing the message, the push notification service attempts to deliver it until the delivery succeeds. If you specify **0**, the message is not stored and delivery is attempted only once. If this delivery fails, the message is discarded.

5. For **Action**, select the action you want to occur if the user opens the notification:

- **Open app** – Your app launches, or it becomes the foreground app if it has been sent to the background.

- **Go to URL** – The default mobile browser on the user's device launches and opens a web page at the URL you specify. For example, this action can be useful for sending users to a blog post.

- **Deep link** – Your app opens and displays a designated user interface. Deep link is an iOS and Android feature. For example, this action can be useful to direct users to special promotions for in-app purchases.

6. (Optional) In the **Media URLs** section, you can optionally provide URLs that point to media files that are displayed in your push notification. The URLs must be publicly accessible so that the push notification services for Android or iOS can retrieve the images.

7. If you are creating an A/B test for the campaign message, complete steps under *Creating a Message A/B Test*. Otherwise, choose **Next step**.

Writing an Email Message

If you chose **Email** as the channel type, write the email that your campaign sends to your user segment.

1. If you previously saved a template that you want to use for your message, load it by choosing **Load template**. The **Subject** and **Message** are populated with the contents of the template.

2. For **Subject**, type the subject for your email.

3. For **Message**, type the email body. You can use the rich text editor to format your message:

To write your message body as HTML, choose the source icon:

When you finish writing your message, you can save it as a template for later use by choosing **Save as template**.

4. (Optional) Under **Plain text message**, type a version of your message for email clients that accept only plain text emails.

5. If you are creating an A/B test for the campaign message, complete steps under *Creating a Message A/B Test*. Otherwise, choose **Next step**.

Writing an SMS Message

If you selected **SMS** as the channel type, write the text message that your campaign sends to your user segment.

1. If you previously saved a template that you want to use for your message, load it by choosing **Load template**. The **Message** is populated with the contents of the template.

2. For **Message type**, choose one of the following:

- **Promotional** – Noncritical messages, such as marketing messages. Amazon Pinpoint optimizes the message delivery to incur the lowest cost.

- **Transactional** – Critical messages that support customer transactions, such as one-time passcodes for multi-factor authentication. Amazon Pinpoint optimizes the message delivery to achieve the highest reliability.

   This campaign-level setting overrides your default message type, which you set on the **Settings** page.

3. For **Message**, type the message body.

   Your text message can have up to 160 characters. A character counter below the right edge of the field counts down from 160 as you enter the text of the message.

   When you finish writing your message, you can save it as a template for later use by choosing **Save as template**.

4. (Optional) For **Sender ID**, type a custom ID that contains up to 11 alphanumeric characters, including at least one letter and no spaces. The sender ID is displayed as the message sender on the receiving device. For example, you can use your business brand to make the message source easier to recognize.

   Support for sender IDs varies by country and/or region. For more information, see Supported Countries and Regions.

   This message-level sender ID overrides your default sender ID, which you set on the **Settings** page.

5. If you are creating an A/B test for the campaign message, complete steps under *Creating a Message A/B Test*. Otherwise, choose **Next step**.

Creating a Message A/B Test

For a campaign that includes an A/B test of the message, define two or more message treatments.

1. To help you start, Amazon Pinpoint provides two treatments. If you want more treatments, choose **Add more**.

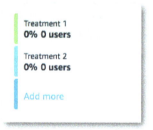

2. For each treatment, do the following:

   1. Customize the treatment name to make it easy to recognize later.

   2. Define the message settings and write the message content.

   3. Set the **Treatment allocation** to specify the percentage of users in the segment who will receive the message for the treatment.

      As you set the allocation for each treatment, the **Holdout** value adjusts to represent the total percentage of users who will not receive messages delivered by this campaign.

3. When you finish defining your treatments, choose **Next step**.

Message Templates

To save your message and reuse it in a separate campaign or direct message, choose **Save as template** and provide a template name. Then, you can load the template for any message by choosing **Load template** and selecting it from a list of saved templates. Amazon Pinpoint populates your message with the template's content. Then, you can send the message as-is or customize as needed.

You can base a template on any supported message type, and you can use the same template for other message types. For example, you can write a push notification message, save it as a template, and use that template for an SMS message. Note that if you use a single template for multiple message types, Amazon Pinpoint loads the content differently for each type. For example, if you base a template on a mobile push message, and you load this template for an email message, the push notification *title* is used as the email *subject*. The correlations between message parts are as follows:

Mobile push templates

The mobile push . . .	Is used as the email . . .	Is used as the SMS . . .
Title	Subject	Not used
Message body	Plain text message	Message body

Email templates

The email . . .	Is used as the mobile push . . .	Is used as the SMS . . .
Subject	Title	Not used
Message body (HTML)	Not used	Not used
Plain text message	Message body	Message body

SMS templates

The SMS . . .	Is used as the mobile push . . .	Is used as the email . . .
Message type	Title	Subject
Message body	Message body	Plain text message

Email Template Restrictions

Email templates can only include the HTML elements and attributes listed in the following table.

Allowed Elements	Allowed Attributes
a	dir, href, style, title
b	dir, style, title
blockquote	cite, dir, style, title
br	dir, style, title
caption	dir, style, title
cite	dir, style, title
code	dir, style, title
col	dir, span, style, title
colgroup	dir, span, style, title
dd	dir, style, title
div	dir, style, title
dl	dir, style, title
dt	dir, style, title
em	dir, style, title

69

Allowed Elements	Allowed Attributes
h1	dir, style, title
h2	dir, style, title
h3	dir, style, title
h4	dir, style, title
h5	dir, style, title
h6	dir, style, title
i	dir, style, title
img	alt, dir, height, src, style, title, width
li	dir, style, title, value
ol	dir, reversed, start, style, title, type
p	dir, style, title
pre	dir, style, title
q	cite, dir, style, title
small	dir, style, title
span	dir, style, title
strike	dir, style, title
strong	dir, style, title
sub	dir, style, title
sup	dir, style, title
table	dir, style, title
tbody	dir, style, title
td	colspan, dir, rowspan, style, title
tfoot	dir, style, title
th	abbr, colspan, dir, rowspan, scope, sorted, style, title
thead	dir, style, title
tr	dir, style, title
u	dir, style, title
ul	dir, style, title

Additionally, some attributes—such as `src` or `href`—allow you to specify a protocol. If your HTML templates include these attributes, they can only specify certain protocols. The allowed protocols for these attributes are listed in the following table.

Element/attribute	Allowed protocols
	ftp, http, https, mailto
	http, https
	http, https
	http, https

Message Variables

To create a message that is personalized for each recipient, use message variables. Message variables refer to specific *endpoint* attributes. These attributes can include characteristics that you add to the endpoint resource, such as the recipient's name, city, device, or operating system. When Amazon Pinpoint sends the message, it substitutes the variables with the corresponding attribute values for the receiving endpoint.

For the attributes, see Endpoint Attributes.

To include a variable in your message, enclose the attribute name in double brackets, as in `{{Demographic. AppVersion}}`.

Often, the most useful endpoint attribute for message variables is `{{Attributes.customAttributeName}}`, where `customAttributeName` refers to custom attributes that you add to the endpoint. By using custom attributes for your variables, you can display personalized messages that are unique for each recipient.

For example, if your app is a fitness app for runners and it includes custom attributes for the user's name, activity, and personal record, you could use variables in the following message:

`Hey {{Attributes.userName}}, congratulations on your new {{Attributes.activity}} PR of {{ Attributes.personalRecord}}!`

When Amazon Pinpoint delivers this message, the content varies for each recipient after the variables are substituted. Possible final messages are:

`Hey Jane Doe, congratulations on your new half marathon PR of 1:42:17!`

Or:

`Hey John Doe, congratulations on your new 5K PR of 20:52!`

For examples of custom attributes for your app's code, see the iOS example or the Android example.

Next
Step 4: Set the Campaign Schedule

Step 4: Set the Campaign Schedule

Schedule when and how often the campaign sends your message to your segment. By default, a campaign sends its message just once on the date and time you choose.

You create a recurring campaign by selecting a **Frequency**, which sets the time interval between successive deliveries of the message. A recurring campaign runs for a fixed duration, beginning and ending when you specify.

If you chose to create a standard campaign, you set only one schedule. After you launch the campaign, you can change any of the schedule's settings except for the frequency.

If you chose to create an A/B test for your campaign's schedule, you define two or more *treatments*, which are variations of the schedule that apply to different portions of the segment. You cannot revise your treatments after you launch the campaign.

Prerequisite
Before you begin, complete Step 3: Write the Message.

To set a schedule

1. Select the frequency with which the campaign runs. The default selection is once, but you can choose a recurring frequency (such as **Weekly**), or you can choose **Immediate** to send the message when you launch the campaign.

2. Unless you are sending the message immediately, choose when the message is sent:

   - If you chose to send the message only once, for **When**, select the date, time, and time zone.

   - If you chose a recurring frequency, for **Start**, select the date, time, and time zone for the beginning of the campaign. The default date is the current date and the default time is immediately (approximately 15 minutes from the current time). For **End**, select a date and time to end the campaign.

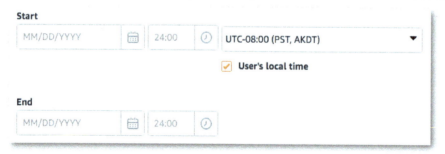

3. Enable **User's local time** if you want to make the schedule take effect according to each recipient's local time. For example, if the campaign start time is 2:00 PM, and the time zone is UTC-05:00 (Eastern Standard Time), then recipients in New York receive the message at 2:00 PM in their local time. One hour later, when the campaign sends its message for UTC-06:00 (Central Standard Time), users in Kansas City receive the message at 2:00 PM in their local time.

   Disable **User's local time** if you want all recipients to receive the message simultaneously, regardless of their local time. For example, this can be useful if you want to send a critical alert to all of your organization's employees at the same moment.

4. For **Quiet Time Start** and **Quiet Time End**, set the time interval during which your campaign sends no messages. For example, set a quiet time to ensure users receive no messages at night. The quiet time

takes effect in each user's local time, regardless of whether the **User's local time** option is disabled.

5. If you are creating an A/B test for the campaign schedule, use the following steps. Otherwise, choose **Next step** to move on to the final step.

To create a schedule A/B test

1. To help you start, Amazon Pinpoint provides two treatments. If you want more treatments, choose **Add more**.

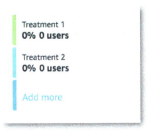

2. For each treatment, do the following:

   1. Customize the treatment name to make it easy to recognize later.

   2. Set the schedule.

   3. Set the **Treatment Allocation** to specify the percentage of users in the segment who will receive messages according to the treatment's schedule.

      As you set the allocation for each treatment, the **Holdout** value adjusts to represent the total percentage of users who will not receive messages delivered by the campaign.

3. When you are finished defining your treatments, choose **Next step**.

Next
Step 5: Review and Launch the Campaign

Step 5: Review and Launch the Campaign

Before you launch the campaign, review your settings and make changes if needed.

Prerequisite
Before you begin, complete Step 4: Set the Campaign Schedule.

To review and launch a campaign

1. For the **Review and launch** step, review the campaign settings. If you need to make changes, choose an earlier stage in the campaign creation process.

2. If all of the settings are correct, choose **Launch campaign**. The console displays the **Campaign details** page for your campaign.

After you launch the campaign, it runs according to the schedule specified. You can monitor campaign analytics to measure the success of the campaign, and you can manage the campaign from its details page.

Managing Campaigns

Using Amazon Pinpoint, you can pause a campaign to suspend message deliveries, update its settings, copy it to make a new campaign, and more.

To manage a campaign

1. Sign in to the AWS Management Console and open the Amazon Pinpoint console at https://console.aws. amazon.com/pinpoint/.

2. On the **Projects** page, choose the project for which you want to manage campaigns.

3. In the navigation menu, choose **Campaigns**.

4. On the **Campaigns** page, choose the campaign that you want to manage.

On the **Campaign details** page, you can do the following:

- **Pause** – Stop sending messages until you resume the campaign. This option is available only for recurring campaigns that you created.

- **Copy to new campaign** – Copy the campaign to use its settings as a template for a new campaign, in which you can change or keep any of the original settings.

- **Edit campaign** – Change the campaign's settings, such as the campaign name, the segment to which it sends messages, the message it delivers, and schedule settings (except for the frequency). If you are editing an A/B test campaign, you cannot edit the message or schedule treatments.

- **Delete campaign** – Remove the campaign from Amazon Pinpoint and stop sending messages through the campaign.

- View **Campaign analytics** – Go to the **Analytics** page to view analytics for the campaign.

Direct Messages with Amazon Pinpoint

With Amazon Pinpoint, you can send a *direct message*, which is a one time message that you send to a limited audience without creating a campaign. Sending a direct message is useful if, before creating a campaign, you want to test how your message appears to recipients.

You can send the message to up to 15 recipients. You cannot use the message to engage a segment. When you send the message, Amazon Pinpoint delivers it immediately, and you cannot schedule the delivery. To engage a user segment, and to schedule the message delivery, create a campaign instead of sending a direct message.

You can send a direct messages using any channel that is supported by Amazon Pinpoint: mobile push, email, or SMS.

Send direct messages by using the **Direct** page in the Amazon Pinpoint console.

To access the Direct page

1. Sign in to the AWS Management Console and open the Amazon Pinpoint console at https://console.aws. amazon.com/pinpoint/.

2. On the **Projects** page, choose the project for which you want to send a message.

3. In the navigation menu, choose **Direct**.

Sending a Mobile Push Notification

To send a direct push notification, you must use a project in which the mobile push channel is enabled. To create a new project with mobile push support, see Setting up Amazon Pinpoint Mobile Push Channels. To add mobile push support to an existing project, see Managing Mobile Push Channels with Amazon Pinpoint.

You can send push notifications through Apple Push Notification service (APNs), Firebase Cloud Messaging (FCM), or the FCM predecessor, Google Cloud Messaging (GCM).

To send a direct push notification

1. On the **Direct** page, choose **Mobile push**.

2. For **Destination type**, choose one of the following destinations for your message:

   - **Endpoint ID** – Each destination is a unique ID assigned to an Amazon Pinpoint *endpoint* resource.

   - **Device token** – Each destination is a token assigned to the instance of the app that you are messaging. This can be the device token assigned by APNs or the registration token assigned by FCM or GCM.

3. Depending on your selection for **Destination type**, type one or more **Endpoint IDs** or **Device tokens**. You can type up to 15 values. Separate each on its own line.

   If you use device tokens as the destination type, specify tokens assigned only by Apple (APNs) or only by Google (FCM or GCM). Amazon Pinpoint can send the message through only one of these push notification providers in a single delivery.

   If you use endpoint IDs as the destination type, this limitation does not apply, and you can specify endpoint resources that use either push notification provider.

4. For **Service**, specify the push notification service through which you are sending the message: **FCM/GCM** or **APNs**. If you use endpoint IDs as the destination type, Amazon Pinpoint detects the service automatically.

5. If you previously saved a template that you want to use for your message, load it by choosing **Load template**. The **Title** and **Message** are populated with the contents of the template.

6. For **Title**, type the title you want to display above the message.

7. For **Message**, type the message body. A character counter below the right edge of the field counts down from 200 as you enter the text of the message.

   When you finish writing your message, you can save it as a template for later use by choosing **Save as template**.

8. For **Action**, select the action you want to occur if the user opens the notification:

   - **Open app** – Your app launches, or it becomes the foreground app if it has been sent to the background.

   - **Go to URL** – The default mobile browser on the user's device launches and opens a webpage at the URL you specify. For example, this action is useful for sending users to a blog post.

   - **Deep link** – Your app opens and displays a designated user interface within the app. Deep link is an iOS and Android feature. For example, this action is useful to direct users to special promotions for in-app purchases.

9. (Optional) In the **Media URLs** section, provide URLs that point to media files that are displayed in your push notification. The URLs must be publicly accessible so that the push notification services for Android or iOS can retrieve the images.

10. When you finish, choose **Send**.

Sending an Email Message

To send a direct email, you must use a project in which the email channel is enabled. To create a new project with email support, see Setting up the Amazon Pinpoint Email Channel. To add email support to an existing project, see Managing the Amazon Pinpoint Email Channel.

1. On the **Direct** page, choose **Email**.

2. For **Destination type**, choose one of the following destinations for your message:

   - **Endpoint ID** – Each destination is a unique ID assigned to an Amazon Pinpoint *endpoint* resource.

   - **Email address** – Each destination is the recipient's email address.

3. Depending on your selection for **Destination type**, type one or more **Endpoint IDs** or **Email addresses**. You can type up to 15 values. Separate each on its own line.

4. If you previously saved a template that you want to use for your message, load it by choosing **Load template**. The **Subject** and **Message** are populated with the contents of the template.

5. For **Subject**, type the subject for your email.

6. For **Message**, type the email body. You can use the rich text editor to format your message:

   To write your message body as HTML, choose the source icon:

   When you finish writing your message, you can save it as a template for later use by choosing **Save as template**.

7. (Optional) Under **Plain text message**, type a version of your message for email clients that accept only plain text emails.

8. When you finish, choose **Send**.

Sending an SMS Message

To send a direct SMS message, you must use a project in which the SMS channel is enabled. To create a new project with SMS support, see Setting up the Amazon Pinpoint SMS Channel. To add SMS support to an existing project, see Managing the Amazon Pinpoint SMS Channel.

To send a direct SMS message

1. On the **Direct** page, choose **SMS**.

2. For **Destination type**, choose one of the following destinations for your message:

   - **Endpoint ID** – Each destination is a unique ID assigned to an Amazon Pinpoint *endpoint* resource.

   - **Phone number** – Each destination is the recipient's phone number.

3. Depending on your selection for **Destination type**, type one or more **Endpoint IDs** or **Phone numbers**. You can type up to 15 values. Separate each on its own line.

   If you use phone numbers as the destination type, specify each number using E.164 format. E.164 is a standard for the phone number structure used for international telecommunication. Phone numbers that follow this format typically have up to 15 digits, and they are prefixed with the plus character (+) and the country code. For example, a US phone number in E.164 format appears as +1206XXX5550100.

4. For **Message type**, choose one of the following:

   - **Promotional** – Noncritical messages, such as marketing messages. Amazon Pinpoint optimizes the message delivery to incur the lowest cost.

   - **Transactional** – Critical messages that support customer transactions, such as one-time passcodes for multi-factor authentication. Amazon Pinpoint optimizes the message delivery to achieve the highest reliability.

   This message-level setting overrides your default message type, which you set on the **Settings** page.

5. If you previously saved a template that you want to use for your message, load it by choosing **Load template**. The **Message** is populated with the contents of the template.

6. For **Message**, type the message body.

   The character limit for a single SMS message is 160. A character counter below the right edge of the field counts down from 160 as you enter the text of the message.

   When you finish writing your message, you can save it as a template for later use by choosing **Save as template**.

7. (Optional) For **Sender ID**, type a custom ID that contains up to 11 alphanumeric characters, including at least one letter and no spaces. The sender ID is displayed as the message sender on the receiving device. For example, you can use your business brand to make the message source easier to recognize.

   Support for sender IDs varies by country and/or region. For more information, see Supported Countries and Regions.

   This message-level sender ID overrides your default sender ID, which you set on the **Settings** page.

8. When you finish, choose **Send**.

Message Templates

To save your message and reuse it in a separate campaign or direct message, choose **Save as template** and provide a template name. Then, you can load the template for any message by choosing **Load template** and selecting it from a list of saved templates. Amazon Pinpoint populates your message with the template's content. Then, you can send the message as-is or customize as needed.

You can base a template on any supported message type, and you can use the same template for other message types. For example, you can write a push notification message, save it as a template, and use that template for an SMS message. Note that if you use a single template for multiple message types, Amazon Pinpoint loads the content differently for each type. For example, if you base a template on a mobile push message, and you load this template for an email message, the push notification *title* is used as the email *subject*. The correlations between message parts are as follows:

Mobile push templates

The mobile push . . .	Is used as the email . . .	Is used as the SMS . . .
Title	Subject	Not used
Message body	Plain text message	Message body

Email templates

The email . . .	Is used as the mobile push . . .	Is used as the SMS . . .
Subject	Title	Not used
Message body (HTML)	Not used	Not used
Plain text message	Message body	Message body

SMS templates

The SMS . . .	Is used as the mobile push . . .	Is used as the email . . .
Message type	Title	Subject
Message body	Message body	Plain text message

Amazon Pinpoint Analytics

Using the analytics provided by Amazon Pinpoint, you can gain insight into your user base by viewing trends related to user engagement, campaign outreach, revenue, and more.

As users interact with your application, the application can report data to Amazon Pinpoint that you can view to learn about your users' level of engagement, purchase activity, and demographics. For example, you can view charts that show how many users open your app each day, the times at which users open your app, and the revenue generated by your app. By viewing charts about device attributes, you can learn which platforms and devices your app is installed on.

You can monitor campaign analytics to see how your campaigns are performing in aggregate as well as individually. You can follow the total number of push notifications sent, the percentage of push notifications that resulted in opening the app, opt-out rates, and other information. If you created a campaign that includes an A/B test, you can use analytics to compare the effectiveness of the campaign treatments. For example, you can assess whether users are more likely to open your app as a result of a variation on your campaign message.

You can create and monitor funnels to analyze how many users are completing each step in a conversion process, such as purchasing an item or upgrading your app.

To analyze or store the analytics data outside of Amazon Pinpoint, you can configure Amazon Pinpoint to stream the data to Amazon Kinesis.

To report metrics from your mobile app, your app must be integrated with Amazon Pinpoint through one of the supported AWS Mobile SDKs. For more information, see Integrating Amazon Pinpoint With Your App in the *Amazon Pinpoint Developer Guide.*

- Chart Reference for Amazon Pinpoint Analytics
- Funnel Analytics
- Streaming App and Campaign Events with Amazon Pinpoint

Chart Reference for Amazon Pinpoint Analytics

On the **Analytics** page, Amazon Pinpoint provides an **overview** of key metrics, and it provides details for **campaigns**, **demographics**, **funnels**, **usage**, **revenue**, and **users**. For further analysis, you can choose any **event** that is reported by your app to see related trends.

Note

Some charts on the **Analytics** page provide data about *endpoints*, and other charts provide data about *users*. An endpoint represents a destination to which you can send messages, such as a user's mobile device, email address, or phone number. Before you can see data about endpoints, your application must register endpoints with Amazon Pinpoint, or you must import your endpoint definitions.

A user represents an individual who is assigned a unique user ID, and this ID is assigned to one or more endpoints. For example, if an individual uses your app on multiple devices, your app could assign that person's user ID to the endpoint for each device. Before you can see data about users, your application must assign user IDs to endpoints, or you must import endpoint definitions that include user IDs.

For information about registering endpoints and assigning user IDs within your mobile app, see Registering Endpoints (iOS) or Registering Endpoints (Android) in the *Amazon Pinpoint Developer Guide*.

For information about registering endpoints and assigning user IDs using the AWS SDK for Java, see Adding Endpoints in the *Amazon Pinpoint Developer Guide*.

For information about importing endpoint definitions, see Importing Segments.

- Overview Charts
- Campaigns Charts
- Demographics Charts
- Events Charts
- Usage Charts
- Revenue Charts
- Users Charts

Overview Charts

The charts on the **Overview** tab summarize metrics related to user engagement and campaigns.

Active targetable endpoints
User endpoints that were active in the previous 30 days, where users have not opted out of notifications.

Campaigns
Open rate – Percentage of recipients who opened your app after receiving a push notification from a campaign.
Delivered – Messages that were successfully sent to the push notification services for iOS and Android.
Active campaigns – Campaigns that are scheduled to start, pending their next run, or currently running. Does not include campaigns that are complete, paused, or deleted.

Daily active endpoints
User endpoints that are active on a specific day.

Monthly active endpoints
Users endpoints that were active in the previous 30 days.

Revenue
Revenue that is reported by your app.

New endpoints
User endpoints that were registered with Amazon Pinpoint for the first time.

Sessions
Number of times your app was opened.

7-day retention rate
Out of the users who opened your app 8 days ago, the percentage who opened it again in the following 7 days.

Campaigns Charts

The charts on the **Campaigns** tab provide the following aggregate information from all of the campaigns for the app.

Active users
Users who opened your app in the previous 30 days.

Delivered
Messages that were successfully sent to the push notification services for iOS and Android.

Open rate
Percentage of recipients who opened your app after receiving a push notification from a campaign.

Opt out rate
Percentage of users who chose not to receive push notifications for your app.

Each campaign for the app is summarized with the following metrics.

Type
Standard – Sends a customized push notification to a specified segment.
A/B test – Includes 2 or more treatments for the message or schedule.

Schedule
The frequency with which the campaign sends push notifications.

User devices messaged
User devices to which the campaign sent push notifications.

Delivered
Messages that were successfully sent to the push notification services for iOS and Android.

Open rate
Percentage of recipients who opened your app after receiving a push notification from a campaign.

Individual Campaign Charts – Standard

In addition to the aggregate analytics for all campaigns on the **Campaigns** tab, you can view the analytics for an individual campaign. The **Analytics** page provides the following information for a standard campaign.

Delivery metrics
Open rate – Percentage of recipients who opened your app after receiving a push notification from a campaign.
Delivery rate – Percentage of the campaign's delivery attempts that were successfully sent to the push notification services for iOS and Android.
User devices messaged – User devices to which the campaign sent push notifications.

Campaign session heat map
The days and times at which users opened your app from a push notification sent by the campaign. Darker colors represent greater numbers of users. Times are based on each user's local time.

Campaign metrics
Sent – Attempted push notification deliveries.
Delivered – Messages that were successfully sent to the push notification services for iOS and Android.
Direct opened – The number of times users opened your app from a push notification sent by the campaign.

Sessions per endpoint
Average number of app sessions started by each user since the start of the campaign.
Average number of times a user endpoint was active since the start of the campaign.

Purchases per endpoint
Average number of in-app purchases made per user endpoint since the start of the campaign.

For a campaign that has delivered messages at least once, the run history is summarized with the following metrics.

Targeted
User devices to which Amazon Pinpoint attempted to deliver messages.

Delivered
The number of successful message deliveries.

Delivery rate
The percentage of all delivery attempts that were successful.

Total opened
The number of app openings resulting from users tapping the notifications sent by the campaign.

Open rate
The percentage of app openings resulting from users tapping the notifications sent by the campaign.

Individual Campaign Charts – A/B Test

For a campaign that includes an A/B test, you can use the campaign's **Analytics** page to compare the effectiveness of the campaign treatments.

Treatment comparisons
Name – Custom name assigned to the treatment.
Allocation – Percentage of users in the campaign's segment who are engaged by the treatment.
Sessions per user – Average number of app sessions started by each user engaged by the treatment since the start of the campaign.
Purchases per user – Average number of purchases from each user engaged by the treatment since the start of the campaign.
vs Holdout – Difference between the *per user* metric and the same metric for users who belong to the campaign's holdout. For example, if, on average, the users engaged by the treatment start 10 app sessions, and the users who belong to the holdout start 5 app sessions, the vs holdout value is **+5**.

Campaign session heat map
The days and times at which users opened your app from a push notification sent by the campaign. Darker colors represent greater numbers of users. Times are based on each user's local time.

Demographics Charts

The charts on the **Demographics** tab provide the characteristics of the devices on which your app is installed. If your app reports custom metrics, those are also displayed.

Platforms
Device platforms on which your app is installed.

App versions
Versions of your app installed on your users' devices.

Models
Device models on which your app is installed.

Makes
Device makes on which your app is installed.

Countries
Countries or regions where your users are located.

Custom charts
Custom attributes reported by your app.

Events Charts

On the **Events** tab, you can choose any event that is reported by your app to see related trends.

Event count
Events reported by your app that match the selected event type and attributes.

Events per session
Average number of matching events that occur in each app session.

Endpoint count
User endpoints that are reporting the selected event.

Usage Charts

The charts on the **Usage** tab indicate how frequently your app is being used and how successfully it retains user interest over time.

Purchases
Number of times purchases were made from your app.

Sessions
Number of times your app was opened.

Sessions per endpoint
Average number of times each user endpoint was active.

Sticky factor
Fraction of monthly active endpoints that were active on a specific day. For example, a sticky factor of .25 means that on a specific day, 25% of active user endpoints from the previous 30 days were active that day.

Session heat map
The days and times at which user endpoints were active based on each user's local time. Darker colors represent greater numbers of active endpoints.

Revenue Charts

The charts on the **Revenue** tab provide details about user purchase activity and the revenue that is generated by your app.

Revenue
Total spent within your app by all users.

Revenue per user
The average revenue from each app user.

Paying users
Users who made one or more purchases by using your app.

Revenue per paying user
The average revenue from each paying user.

Units sold
Total items purchased within your app by all users.

Revenue per unit sold
The average revenue from each unit sold.

Purchases
Number of times users made a purchase by using your app.

Units per purchase
The average number of units sold with each purchase.

Users Charts

The charts on the **Users** tab provide app usage metrics for endpoints and users, and they provide metrics about user authentication. For example, a user who uses your app on multiple devices counts as one user in the **Daily Active Users** chart, but each of the user's devices counts as one endpoint in the **Daily Active Endpoints** chart.

You can enable several of the metrics on this tab by using Amazon Cognito user pools to manage user authentication. User pools provide user directories that make it easier to add sign-up and sign-in to your app. As users authenticate with your app, Amazon Cognito reports data to Amazon Pinpoint, including sign-ups, sign-ins, failed authentications, daily active users, and monthly active users. For more information, see Using Amazon Pinpoint Analytics with Amazon Cognito User Pools in the *Amazon Cognito Developer Guide*.

If you don't want to use Amazon Cognito user pools, to view analytics about users, you must assign user IDs to your endpoint definitions. To view analytics about user authentication, your app must report the supported authentication event types to Amazon Pinpoint.

Daily active users
Users who opened your app on a specific day.

Daily active endpoints
User endpoints active on a specific day.

Monthly active users
Users who opened your app in the previous 30 days.

Monthly active endpoints
User endpoints active in the previous 30 days.

Active users month-to-date
Users who opened your app after the start of the current calendar month.

Sign-ins
Number of times users signed in to your app.

Sign-ups
Number of times users signed up for your app.

Authentication failures
Number of failed authentication calls.

Funnel Analytics

You can use Amazon Pinpoint to analyze *funnels*, which visualize how many users complete each of a series of steps in your app. For example, the series of steps in a funnel can be a conversion process that results in a purchase (as in a shopping cart), or some other intended user behavior.

By monitoring funnels, you can assess whether conversion rates have improved because of changes made to your app or because of an Amazon Pinpoint campaign.

After you specify which steps belong in your funnel, the **Create funnel** page displays a chart like the following example:

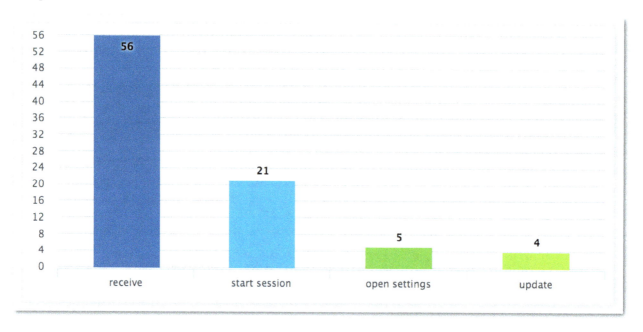

This example chart shows the percentage of users who complete each step in the process of updating an app. By comparing the values between columns, you can determine the drop off rates between steps. In this example, there is a 35% drop off between users who receive a notification and those who start an app session. Then there is a 19% drop off between users who start a session and those who open the app settings page.

To create a funnel, you specify each event that is part of the conversion process you want to analyze. Your app reports these events to Amazon Pinpoint as long as it integrates Amazon Mobile Analytics through one of the supported AWS SDKs. If your app is a project in AWS Mobile Hub, you integrate Amazon Mobile Analytics by enabling the App Analytics feature in the AWS Mobile Hub console.

When you add events to your funnel, you can choose any event that is reported by your app. Your app can report the following types of events:

- Standard events – Includes events that automatically report when an app session starts or stops. The event type names for standard events are denoted with an underscore prefix, as in `_session.start`. Standard events also include monetization events that report in-app purchases.

- Custom events – Defined by you to monitor activities specific to your app, such as completing a level in a game, posting to social media, or setting particular app preferences.

For information about creating events using the AWS Mobile SDK for Android or the AWS Mobile SDK for iOS, see Generating Mobile Analytics Events in the *Amazon Mobile Analytics User Guide*.

To create a funnel

1. Sign in to the AWS Management Console and open the Amazon Pinpoint console at https://console.aws. amazon.com/pinpoint/.

2. On the Amazon Pinpoint homepage, choose the app for which you want to create a funnel.

3. On the **Analytics** page, choose **Funnels**. The **Funnels** page opens, and it displays any previously defined funnels.

4. Choose **Create funnel**.

5. For **Funnel name**, type a custom name to make the funnel easy to recognize later.

6. To create the funnel, specify the events that you want to add to the funnel chart. For each event, specify the following:

   - **Name** – A name for the funnel chart.

   - **Event** – The event type reported by your app to Amazon Pinpoint.

   - **Attributes** – The attribute-value pairs that are assigned to the events you want to add to the chart.

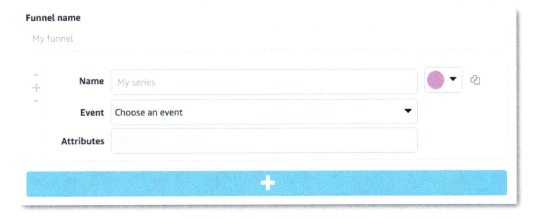

7. To add more events, choose the add (+) button, or copy an event by choosing the copy icon.

Streaming App and Campaign Events with Amazon Pinpoint

Amazon Pinpoint can stream app usage and campaign engagement data, known as *events*, to supported AWS services, which provide more options for analysis and storage.

After you integrate your app with Amazon Pinpoint, it reports app events, such as the number of app sessions started by users. Amazon Pinpoint provides this data in the analytics charts for that app in the console. The analytics charts also show campaign events generated by Amazon Pinpoint, such as the number of devices the campaign sent messages to.

Amazon Pinpoint retains this data for 90 days; however, you can't directly access it for custom analysis. To keep this data for an indefinite period of time, or to analyze it with custom queries and tools, you can configure Amazon Pinpoint to send events to Kinesis.

- About Amazon Kinesis
- Streaming Amazon Pinpoint Events to Kinesis

About Amazon Kinesis

The Kinesis platform offers services that you can use to load and analyze streaming data on AWS. You can configure Amazon Pinpoint to send app and campaign events to Amazon Kinesis Data Streams or Amazon Kinesis Data Firehose. By streaming your events, you enable more flexible options for data analysis, such as:

- Converging the events from multiple apps into one stream so that you can analyze this data as a collection.

- Analyzing events with AWS query services. For example, you can use Amazon Kinesis Data Analytics to execute SQL queries against streaming data.

About Amazon Kinesis Data Streams

Amazon Kinesis Data Streams is a service that you can use to build custom applications that process or analyze your streaming data. For example, streaming your events to Kinesis Data Streams is useful if you want to use event data in your custom dashboards, generate alerts based on events, or dynamically respond to events.

For more information, see the Amazon Kinesis Data Streams Developer Guide.

About Amazon Kinesis Data Firehose

Amazon Kinesis Data Firehose is a service that you can use to deliver your streaming data to AWS data stores, including Amazon Simple Storage Service (Amazon S3), Amazon Redshift, or Amazon Elasticsearch Service. For example, streaming your events to Kinesis Data Firehose is useful if you want to:

- Use your own analytics applications and tools to analyze events in Amazon S3, Amazon Redshift, or Amazon Elasticsearch Service.

- Send your events to Amazon S3 so that you can write SQL queries on this data with Amazon Athena.

- Back up your event data for long-term storage in Amazon S3.

For more information, see the Amazon Kinesis Data Firehose Developer Guide.

Streaming Amazon Pinpoint Events to Kinesis

The Kinesis platform offers services that you can use to load and analyze streaming data on AWS. You can configure Amazon Pinpoint to send app and campaign events to Amazon Kinesis Data Streams for processing in external applications or third-party analytics tools. You can also configure Amazon Pinpoint to stream this event data to AWS datastores (such as Amazon Redshift) using Amazon Kinesis Data Firehose.

Prerequisites

Before you complete the procedure in this section, create either an Amazon Kinesis stream or a Kinesis Data Firehose delivery stream in the same account in which you use Amazon Pinpoint. To learn more about creating Kinesis streams, see Kinesis Streams in the *Amazon Kinesis Data Streams Developer Guide*. To learn more about creating Kinesis Data Firehose delivery streams, see Creating an Amazon Kinesis Data Firehose Delivery Stream in the *Amazon Kinesis Data Firehose Developer Guide*.

You can optionally create an IAM role that grants permission to send data to your stream. If you do not create this role, Amazon Pinpoint can create one for you. For more information about creating this policy manually, see Permissions Policies in the *Amazon Pinpoint Developer Guide*.

Setting up Event Streaming

Complete the following steps in Amazon Pinpoint to set up event streaming.

To set up event streaming

1. Sign in to the AWS Management Console and open the Amazon Pinpoint console at https://console.aws.amazon.com/pinpoint/.

2. On the **Projects** page, choose the app for which you want to set up data streaming.

3. In the navigation pane on the left, choose **Settings**.

4. On the **Settings** page, choose **Event stream**.

5. Select the box next to **Enable streaming of events to Amazon Kinesis**.

6. Under **Stream to Amazon Kinesis**, choose one of the following options:

   - **Send events to an Amazon Kinesis stream** – choose this option if you want to send Amazon Pinpoint event data to an external application for analysis.

   - **Send events to an Amazon Kinesis Data Firehose delivery stream** – choose this option if you want to send event data to an AWS datastore, such as Amazon Redshift.

7. For **Amazon Kinesis stream** or **Amazon Kinesis Data Firehose delivery stream**, choose the Amazon Kinesis stream that you want to use to export the data. **Note**
   If you have not yet created the Amazon Kinesis stream, open the Amazon Kinesis console at https://console.aws.amazon.com/kinesis. For more information about creating streams, see the Amazon Kinesis Data Streams Developer Guide or the Amazon Kinesis Data Firehose Developer Guide.

8. Under IAM role, choose one of the following options:

   - **Automatically create a role** – choose this option to automatically create an IAM role with the required permissions. This role authorizes Amazon Pinpoint to send data to the stream you chose in step 6.

   - **Choose a role from your account** – choose this option to have Amazon Pinpoint assume an IAM role that already exists in your account. The role you select must allow the `firehose:PutRecordBatch` action. For an example of a policy that allows this action, see Permissions Policies in the *Amazon Pinpoint Developer Guide*.

9. Choose **Save**.

As Amazon Pinpoint receives events from your app and generates campaign events, it sends this data to your Kinesis stream. For more information about the data that Amazon Pinpoint sends for an event, see Event Data in the *Amazon Pinpoint Developer Guide*.

Amazon Pinpoint Settings

Manage settings to tailor Amazon Pinpoint for your messaging use cases and requirements. You can control aspects of your app users' experience, and you customize Amazon Pinpoint for your business needs.

Manage account settings to configure SMS messaging options that take effect for all of your Amazon Pinpoint projects. Account settings include your monthly SMS spending limit, sender ID, two-way SMS response messages, and more.

Manage project settings to specify the default settings for an individual project, including the frequency with which your app users receive messages and the times at which they receive messages.

- Managing Account Settings in Amazon Pinpoint
- Managing Project Settings in Amazon Pinpoint

Managing Account Settings in Amazon Pinpoint

Use the **Account settings** page in the Amazon Pinpoint console to manage account-level SMS settings that take effect for all of your Amazon Pinpoint projects. The settings include SMS spending limits, your default sender ID, automated keyword responses, and two-way SMS options.

Many of the SMS settings on this page are unavailable until you contact AWS Support. For example, you must submit a case with AWS Support if you want to increase your spend limit, reserve a dedicated origination number, or reserve a custom sender ID. For more information, see Requesting Support for SMS Messaging with Amazon Pinpoint.

Because these settings apply to your AWS account, some settings also take effect for Amazon SNS, an AWS service that you can also use to send SMS messages.

To manage your account settings, sign in to the AWS Management Console, and open the Amazon Pinpoint console at https://console.aws.amazon.com/pinpoint/. Then, on the **Projects** page, choose **Account settings**.

Under **SMS**, configure your general SMS settings, and configure the number settings for your short codes and long codes.

General SMS Settings

Specify your general SMS preferences, such as your default message type and your monthly spending limit.

To configure general SMS settings

1. Under **General**, for **Default message type**, select the type of SMS message that you will usually send:

   - **Promotional** – Noncritical messages, such as marketing messages. Amazon Pinpoint optimizes the message delivery for lowest cost.

   - **Transactional** – Critical messages that support customer transactions, such as one-time passcodes for multi-factor authentication. Amazon Pinpoint optimizes the message delivery for highest reliability.

   You can override this setting when you send a message.

   For pricing information for promotional and transactional messages, see Amazon Pinpoint Pricing.

2. For **Account spending limit**, type the maximum amount, in USD, that you want to spend on SMS messages each calendar month. When Amazon Pinpoint determines that sending an SMS message would incur a cost that exceeds your spend limit for that month, Amazon Pinpoint stops publishing SMS messages within minutes. **Important**
   Because Amazon Pinpoint is a distributed system, it stops sending SMS messages within a time interval of minutes of the spend limit being exceeded. During that interval, if you continue to send SMS messages, you might incur costs that exceed your limit.

   By default, the spend limit is 1.00 USD. To request a limit increase, see Requesting Increases to Your Monthly SMS Spend Threshold for Amazon Pinpoint.

3. For **Default sender ID**, type a custom ID that contains up to 11 alphanumeric characters, including at least one letter and no spaces. The sender ID is displayed as the message sender on the receiving device. For example, you can use your business brand to make the message source easier to recognize.

   Support for sender IDs varies by country and/or region. For more information, see Supported Countries and Regions.

   To request a dedicated sender ID, see Requesting Sender IDs for SMS Messaging with Amazon Pinpoint.

   You can override this setting when you send a message.

4. Choose **Save**.

Number Settings

Manage settings for the dedicated *short codes* and *long codes* that you have requested from AWS Support and that are assigned to your account.

A short code is a 5 or 6 digit number that is meant for high-volume SMS messaging. To request a dedicated short code, see Requesting Dedicated Short Codes for SMS Messaging with Amazon Pinpoint.

A long code is a standard 10 digit phone number that is meant for low-volume, person-to-person communication. To request a dedicated long code, see Requesting Dedicated Long Codes for SMS Messaging with Amazon Pinpoint.

After you receive one or more dedicated short codes or long codes from AWS, those numbers are provided under **Number settings**, where you can manage settings for keywords and two-way SMS.

Keyword Settings

A *keyword* is a specific word or phrase that your audience can text to your number to elicit a response, such as an informational message or a special offer. When your number receives a message that begins with a keyword, Amazon Pinpoint responds with a customizable message.

For short codes, the console shows the keywords and responses that you initially define when you request a short code from AWS Support. AWS Support registers your keywords and responses with the wireless carriers when provisioning your short code.

For long codes, the console shows the default keywords and responses.

Important
Your keywords and response messages must comply with guidelines set by wireless carriers and wireless industry groups. Otherwise, following an audit, such groups might take action against your short code or long code. This action can include blacklisting your number and blocking your messages.

Default Keywords

The following keywords are required by wireless carriers in the US for short codes, and they are expected by AWS for all long codes and short codes:

HELP
Used to obtain customer support. The response message must include customer support contact information, as in the following example:
"For assistance with your account, call 1 (NNN) 555-0199"

STOP
Used to opt out of receiving messages from your number. In addition to STOP, your audience can use any supported opt-out keyword, such as CANCEL or OPTOUT. For all opt-out keywords, see SMS Opt Out. After your number receives an opt-out keyword, Amazon Pinpoint stops sending SMS messages from your account to the individual who opted out.
The response message must confirm that messages are no longer sent to the individual who opted out, as in the following example:
"You are now opted out and will no longer receive messages."

Registered Keyword

A required custom keyword that is specific to your SMS use case. For example, your audience might text the keyword DISCOUNT to your short code, and the response message could include a promotional code.

Managing Keyword Settings

Use the Amazon Pinpoint console to customize the keyword responses for your number.

1. On the **Account settings** page, under **Number settings**, choose the short code or long code for which you want to manage keyword responses.

   The **Number settings** page displays. Under **Keywords**, the console provides:

   - The default keywords HELP and STOP. You can edit the response messages, but you cannot edit the keywords.

   - Your registered keyword. If you want to change your registered keyword, you must first open a case with AWS Support and request to update your keyword with the wireless carriers. Then, you must edit the keyword in the Amazon Pinpoint console to match. You can also edit the response message, but the intent of the message must remain consistent with the message that you provide to AWS Support.

2. In the table that contains the keyword you want to edit, choose **Edit**, and edit the keyword and response message as needed.

3. When you finish making your changes, choose **Save**.

Two-Way SMS Settings

Define keywords for messages that you want to receive and process outside of Amazon Pinpoint. When your number receives an SMS message that begins with one of these keywords, Amazon Pinpoint sends the message and related data to an Amazon SNS topic in your account. You can use Amazon SNS to publish the message to topic subscribers or to AWS services for further processing.

To manage two-way SMS settings

1. On the **Account settings** page, under **Number settings**, choose the short code or long code for which you want to manage two-way SMS settings.

2. If you haven't already, choose **Enable 2-way SMS**.

3. Under **Keywords**, you can add or edit keywords and response messages. When your number receives an SMS message that begins with one of these keywords, Amazon Pinpoint does the following:

   - Sends the message to your Amazon SNS topic.

   - Responds with the keyword response message, if specified.

4. Under **Amazon SNS topic**, specify the topic that receives your SMS messages with one of the following options:

   - **Automatically create a topic** – Amazon Pinpoint creates a topic in your account.

   - **Choose a topic from your account** – Specify the ARN of a topic in your account.

5. Choose **Save**.

   If you created an Amazon SNS topic, you can see the topic by going to the Amazon SNS console at https://console.aws.amazon.com/sns/v2/home.

Example Two-Way SMS Message Payload

When your number receives an SMS message that begins with a keyword that you define for two-way SMS, Amazon Pinpoint sends a JSON payload to an Amazon SNS topic that you designate. The JSON payload contains the message and related data, as in the following example:

```json
1 {
2   "originationNumber": "+1XXX5550100",
3   "messageBody": "offers",
4   "inboundMessageId": "cae173d2-66b9-564c-8309-21f858e9fb84",
5   "messageKeyword": "offers",
6   "destinationNumber": "+1XXX5550199"
7 }
```

The value for originationNumber is the number from which the message was sent (your customer's number).
The value for destinationNumber is the number to which the message was sent (your short code or long code).

Managing Project Settings in Amazon Pinpoint

You can use the Amazon Pinpoint console to specify default settings for your project, such as the maximum number of messages that each campaign can deliver to your users.

To manage the default project settings

1. Sign in to the AWS Management Console and open the Amazon Pinpoint console at https://console.aws. amazon.com/pinpoint/.

2. On the **Projects** page, choose the project for which you want to manage settings.

3. In the navigation menu, choose **Settings**.

On the **Settings** page, under the **Project** tab, you can set the following options:

- **Maximum number of messages a user can receive per day** – The number of messages that each campaign for the app can send to each user daily.

- **Maximum number of messages a user can receive for a campaign** – The total number of messages that each campaign for the app can send.

- **Maximum number of messages a campaign can send per second** – The number of messages per second that each campaign can send. The minimum value is 50, and the maximum value is 20,000.

- **Maximum number of seconds a campaign can be running** – The amount of time, in seconds, in which each campaign attempts to deliver a message after its scheduled delivery time. The minimum value is 60.

- **Quiet time** – The default quiet time for the app. Each campaign for this app sends no messages during this time unless the campaign overrides the default with a quiet time of its own.

- **Abbreviated numbers** – Simplifies large numbers in the Amazon Pinpoint console. For example, 10,534,534 will be represented as 10.53 M.

Under the **Event streams** tab, you can configure Amazon Pinpoint to stream app and campaign events to Amazon Kinesis. For more information, see Streaming App and Campaign Events with Amazon Pinpoint.

Under the **Channels** tab, you can manage the settings for your mobile push and email channels, and you can enable the SMS channel for your project. To manage SMS settings, use the **Account settings** page. For more information, see:

- Managing Mobile Push Channels with Amazon Pinpoint

- Updating Email Settings

- Managing Account Settings in Amazon Pinpoint

Document History for Amazon Pinpoint

The following table describes the documentation for this release of Amazon Pinpoint.

- **Latest documentation update:** February 23, 2018

Change	Description	Date
SMS best practices	Added a best practices guide that contains tips and information related to SMS campaigns.	February 23, 2018
Requesting support for SMS use cases	Contact AWS Support to request support for your SMS use case if you want to increase your spending limit, reserve an origination number, or reserve a sender ID.	February 21, 2018
Segment import documentation	Amazon Pinpoint can now create an IAM role for you automatically.	February 6, 2018
Two-way SMS support by country	Updated the table of Supported Countries and Regions for the SMS channel to list the countries and regions that support 2-way SMS.	February 5, 2018
Time to Live value for mobile push	In the Amazon Pinpoint console, you can specify a Time to Live (TTL) value when you write a mobile push message for a campaign.	December 22, 2017
Removal of Amazon S3 export documentation	The ability to export Amazon Pinpoint event data directly to Amazon S3 has been deprecated. Instead, you can use Amazon Kinesis Data Firehose to send event data to Amazon S3, Amazon Redshift, and other AWS services. For more information, see Streaming App and Campaign Events with Amazon Pinpoint.	December 18, 2017
Segment import documentation	Importing Segments includes updated information about how to create endpoint files, the attributes you can use within these files, and how to create an IAM role for importing.	October 26, 2017

Change	Description	Date
APNs token authentication and APNs sandbox support	The APNs channel settings accept a .p8 signing key so that Amazon Pinpoint can construct authentication tokens for your push notifications.Use the APNs channel to send notifications to production and sandbox environments.	September 27, 2017
ADM and Baidu mobile push	Enable mobile push channels for Amazon Device Message and Baidu Cloud Push in your projects.	September 27, 2017
User analytics with Amazon Cognito user pools	To enable analytics about users and authentication, use Amazon Cognito user pools to manage user sign-in.	September 26, 2017
Account settings	Use the Account settings page in the console to manage account-level SMS settings that take effect for all of your projects.	September 11, 2017
Users analytics	Users charts in the Amazon Pinpoint console provide metrics about app usage and user authentication.	August 31, 2017
Direct email messages	You can send email messages directly, to a limited audience, without creating a campaign or engaging a segment.	July 05, 2017
New channels: email and SMS	In addition to the mobile push channel, you can enable email and SMS channels as part of your Amazon Pinpoint projects. With these channels enabled, you can send emails or text messages with your campaigns.	June 08, 2017
Direct messaging	You can send push notifications and text messages directly, to a limited audience, without creating a campaign or engaging a segment.	June 08, 2017
Revenue charts	You can view revenue charts in the Amazon Pinpoint console to see the revenue that is generated by your app and the number of items purchased by users.	March 31, 2017
Event streams	You can configure Amazon Pinpoint to send your app and campaign events to an Kinesis stream.	March 24, 2017

Change	Description	Date
Amazon Pinpoint general availability	This release introduces Amazon Pinpoint.	December 1, 2016

www.ingramcontent.com/pod-product-compliance
Lightning Source LLC
LaVergne TN
LVHW082040050326
832904LV00005B/254